W9-DCV-810

"Every smug or indifferent or self-centered person in America should read this book—and it would help professing Christians, too. It is profound in its understanding of the God with whom we have to deal; it is hard-hitting for a pampered society; it is fascinating reading. A great book in the Multnomah tradition!"

D. JAMES KENNEDY, PH.D.
FOUNDER OF EVANGELISM EXPLOSION
SENIOR MINISTER, CORAL RIDGE PRESBYTERIAN CHURCH

"Whenever a writer tackles the subject of God, my theological sentry snaps to attention. The catechism question about the chief end of man being to glorify God and to enjoy Him forever has been fermenting in human hands and revamped. Man's chief end—and it's a multilane thoroughfare—has now become to glorify man.

"With all the doctrinal traffic racing in man's direction, it takes a well-designed traffic sign to alert drivers of dangers ahead, but that's what Steve Lawson has done in *Made in Our Image*. It's as if Christians are filling up their tanks with the wrong fuel. Instead of hearing what God has to say about Himself, we fill up on cut-rate additives and limp along, losing one spiritual battle after another. This author has erected a service station to prepare believers for the real Christian life-journey.

"Here are pages printed for pondering, words worth chewing on for long-term endurance, and biblical, truth-guarding discussion especially designed for winners in the race of twenty-first-century life."

HOWARD G. HENDRICKS
DISTINGUISHED PROFESSOR AND CHAIRMAN,
CENTER FOR CHRISTIAN LEADERSHIP,
DALLAS THEOLOGICAL SEMINARY

"By recognizing that man is unable to discover God by natural reasoning (1 Corinthians 1:21) and accepting the validity of God's self-revelation as contained in the Scriptures (1 Corinthians 2:10), and by analyzing and synthesizing what the Word reveals about the person and attributes of God, Steve Lawson brings the reader not only an intimate knowledge of God, but also an attitude of humble, worshipful submission to His majesty and glory."

J. DWIGHT PENTECOST
DISTINGUISHED PROFESSOR EMERITUS
OF BIBLE EXPOSITION,
DALLAS THEOLOGICAL SEMINARY

"*Made in Our Image* by Steven J. Lawson is a welcome deterrent to the 'user-friendly,' denigrating view of the person and perfections of our awesome and almighty God. With the clear scriptural mandate for all Christians to 'cease being conformed to this age,' it surely follows with even more urgency that we cease reducing God to our image. I commend my good friend for writing this book and pray for a wide readership and response."

STEPHEN F. OLFORD
FOUNDER AND SENIOR LECTURER,
THE STEPHEN OLFORD CENTER FOR BIBLICAL PREACHING

MADE IN *Our* IMAGE

What Shall We Do with a "User-Friendly" god?

STEVEN J. LAWSON

Multnomah Publishers® *Sisters, Oregon*

MADE IN *OUR* IMAGE
published by Multnomah Publishers, Inc.

© 2000 by Dr. Steven J. Lawson
International Standard Book Number: 1-57673-610-5

Cover illustration by Douglas Klauba
Design by Kirk DouPonce/David Uttley Design

Scripture quotations are from:
New American Standard Bible
© 1960, 1977 by the Lockman Foundation

Also quoted:
The Holy Bible, New King James Version (NKJV)
© 1984 by Thomas Nelson, Inc.

Multnomah is a trademark of Multnomah Publishers, Inc.,
and is registered in the U.S. Patent and Trademark Office.
The colophon is a trademark of Multnomah Publishers, Inc.

Printed in the United States of America

For information:
MULTNOMAH PUBLISHERS, INC.
POST OFFICE BOX 1720
SISTERS, OREGON 97759

00 01 02 03 04 05 — 10 9 8 7 6 5 4 3 2 1 0

This book is gratefully dedicated to
the distinguished faculties of the two
seminaries from which I have graduated:

DALLAS THEOLOGICAL SEMINARY
and
REFORMED THEOLOGICAL SEMINARY

Specifically, I want to express my deepest
appreciation for two gifted professors:

DR. JOHN HANNAH
and
DR. R. C. SPROUL

These men have uniquely marked my life
by imparting to me what is most precious—a high view of God.
Through their teaching ministries in the classroom,
I became overshadowed by the infinite glory of God.
No greater influence could have been brought to bear upon
my life than a transcendent view of Him who is over all.
For this, I shall always be grateful.

The fear of the LORD is the beginning of wisdom,
And the knowledge of
the Holy One is understanding.
PROVERBS 9:10

Contents

Part Three: The Experience of God

FOREWORD

The tendency to treat God like a wax figure who can be reshaped according to human tastes and fashions is certainly nothing new. It is a form of idolatry that has been around at least since Sinai, when the disobedient Israelites portrayed Jehovah as a golden calf. A similar but subtler kind of idolatry is currently having a heyday in the church.

Modern Christians seem plagued with uncertainty about whether the God of Scripture is really relevant in today's world. Some deliberately omit or ignore all the difficult biblical truths about God and seek to portray Him as friendlier or more approachable than they think Scripture does. Others openly advocate "reimagining" God in feminist terms or some other politically correct form.

One of the most intensely debated theological trends today is a doctrine known as "openness" theology. Advocates of this view claim that the future is largely "open"—undetermined—from the divine perspective. In their view, God does not and cannot know the future with certainty or complete accuracy. Thus, in their zeal to humanize God and explain the problem of evil, they have thrown out the biblical doctrine of God. They have redefined divine foreknowledge and omniscience so that, in effect, they have eliminated those concepts from their view of God.

Steve Lawson's *Made in Our Image* is an eye-opening and honest appraisal of how these quests for contemporary notions of God have taken the church away from knowing and understanding the God who has revealed Himself in Scripture. With a simple yet biblical approach, Dr. Lawson sets forth the biblical doctrine of God and His glorious attributes. In the process, he shows how all the modern, "user-friendly" notions about God are really sub-Christian ideas of Him—forms of idolatry, to put it plainly.

Voltaire, the famous French agnostic and author, once quipped, "God created man in His image, and man returned the favor." Unfortunately, Voltaire never spoke more truthfully. Scripture condemns those who have "changed the glory of the uncorruptible God into an image made like to corruptible man" (Romans 1:23). A wrong view of God is not an error to be dismissed lightly.

Made in Our Image is a much-needed resource about a topic that is vital to the health of the church as we enter a new millennium. If we're not accurately proclaiming the God of Scripture, then everything else we say is utterly in vain.

JOHN MACARTHUR,
PASTOR/TEACHER
GRACE COMMUNITY CHURCH
SUN VALLEY, CALIFORNIA

FOREWORD

Many years ago, A. W. Tozer stated it clearly: "What comes into our minds when we think about God is the most important thing about us." The concept of God that comes most quickly to our minds is the most determinative factor of our entire worldview and understanding of reality.

Consciously or unconsciously, we live out our most basic beliefs and reveal what we really believe about God, the world, and ourselves. Even a superficial glance at postmodern America reveals that most persons operate out of an understanding of God that is decidedly unbiblical and unorthodox.

How did this happen? The modern assault on the biblical doctrine of God began when the Enlightenment replaced revelation with reason. Unhindered by Scripture, modern theologians and philosophers progressively redefined God so that the deity was cut down to manageable size—a God even liberals could love.

As modern scientism and skepticism ran their courses, God was stripped of His attributes and robbed of His holiness. Modern theologians ran through a series of liberalizing theologies including deism, unitarianism, process theology, empiricism, and various other movements and fads—all of which rejected the God of the Bible.

Liberal theology began by stressing the love of God while denying His holiness and justice. Before long, all that was left was a weak though good-natured deity, bumbling about and generally hoping that his human creatures would just get along.

Now, even some who call themselves evangelicals are seeking to redefine God. These theologians are calling for an "open" view of God that rejects the classical understanding of God's unlimited power and exhaustive foreknowledge. This understanding of God allows that God may work toward goals, but asserts that He can never be certain of the outcome.

The god of American popular culture is an indulgent heavenly spirit who is little threat to our lifestyles and luxuries—a god consistent with a consumer culture and rampant immorality. This god might wish that human beings would behave, but he is powerless when they do not.

A vast majority of Americans claims to believe in God, but most believe in an idol of their own imaginations. This deity is always there to be called upon in times of trouble, but he would never intrude upon our personal space, judge our sins, or hinder our happiness.

In this book, Steve Lawson describes the idolatrous images of God so popular in our day and points us to the Scriptures for the revelation of the true and living God of the Bible. He rejects the "user-friendly" God of modern sentimentality and shows us the God of Abraham, Isaac, and Jacob. He reviews the distortions of God so common in America, and even in our churches.

Most importantly, Dr. Lawson sets the record straight concerning what the Bible teaches about God—His attributes and His character. He cuts no corners and avoids none of the hard issues. His recovery of the biblical doctrine of God puts him in agreement with the Fathers of the church, the Reformers, the Puritans, and all those who cherish the biblical doctrine of God.

Dr. Lawson writes as a gifted and caring pastor. His pastoral concern is evident in the approach he takes in this book. He knows that our moral lives and our concept of God are inextricably tied together. A biblical understanding of God is absolutely essential to a proper understanding of ourselves, of the Gospel, and of life itself. As Dr. Lawson states, "When your view of God is fuzzy, everything else is distorted. Conversely, a proper vision of God brings everything distinctly into focus."

The anemic view of God held by many church members is evident in doctrinal confusion, corrupted worship, compromised evangelism, and spiritual deadness. The absence of awe, wonder, and exaltation in our worship indicates that we have rejected one of the most critical teachings of Scripture—the fear of God.

Steve Lawson proves that the biblical doctrine of God is far more sublime than that offered by popular culture, liberal theologians, or the evangelical revisionists. He deals with God's sovereignty, wrath, love, holiness, goodness, and glory, as well as the proper understanding of worship and devotion.

Human beings, created in the image of God, have now attempted to imagine God in our own image. Steve Lawson sets the record straight and calls all Christians to embrace without compromise the biblical doctrine of God. *Made in Our Image* is an antidote to modern confusion and a prescription for the illness in the contemporary church. We should consider this book as first aid for a church in a theological emergency.

R. ALBERT MOHLER
PRESIDENT,
SOUTHERN BAPTIST THEOLOGICAL SEMINARY
LOUISVILLE, KENTUCKY

ACKNOWLEDGMENTS

I want to express my gratitude to a small circle of people who have aided in the preparation of this book in various ways. Thanks to:

Tracy Sumner, my editor at Multnomah, who so patiently and cheerfully worked with me in editing this manuscript to make it the best it could be;

Julie Riley and Stephanie Reeves for typing the manuscript;

Jason Allen, my assistant, as well as Bill Eubanks, and Chuck Finster, for reviewing and editing the manuscript.

Jean Steelman and Michael Steelman for their suggestions about grammar;

Anne, my wife, along with our four children, Andrew, James, Grace Anne, and John, who have faithfully prayed for me and graciously sacrificed much of our family time to allow me to write this book.

INTRODUCTION

This is a book about God. Not God as we might loosely imagine Him to be, but God as He truly is—holy, awesome, sovereign, righteous, and full of love and goodness.

I believe that if there is one area of our theology that is most lacking in the church today, it is our understanding of who He really is. Our most rudimentary problem is that we do not fully comprehend who He is. Our thoughts about Him have become very unclear, fuzzy, and oblique. The result of this distorted view of deity is that it leaves everything else out of focus as well. Whenever we lose a right view of God, everything else gets out of perspective.

Sad to say, we are suffering from a low view of God—an impoverished vision of Him as a god with manlike characteristics. A "user-friendly" god has become the trend of the day—a god made in *our* image, an inversion of the truth of man made in His image. Human qualities and finite limitations have been assigned to the One who exceeds our comprehension. Rather than seeing Him as He is—above and beyond us, infinite in His divine perfections—He is portrayed as a glorified *us*.

The result is a god who makes us feel comfortable—one we can control and manage, even use. This downsized version of God is a diminutive deity dependent upon us; we are not dependent upon Him. Forged upon the anvil of a sloppy handling of Scripture and shallow thoughts about God, this user-friendly sovereign is a strange kind of codependent god, and we see the effects of his influence all around us. Many churches have become nothing more than entertainment centers, giving slick performances to growing numbers of mesmerized but unproductive churchgoers. Such devices may bring people into the church, but they do not transform them once they arrive.

Unfortunately, many today are seeking to redefine church, as though this were an option. By looking to the world for a model of what the body of Christ should look like, the modern-day church is suffering an identity crisis of monumental proportions.

This is the tragic legacy of the user-friendly god.

Some see the church as being *consumer driven*. They say we should survey our target market, discover what they want, and then give it to them. Wanting what we offer, people will pack the pews. Quite frankly, this is tantamount to the patient, instead of the doctor, writing his own prescription. Oblivious to his real illness, the patient never finds a cure.

Others see the church as *culture driven*. A slight variation of the consumer-driven model, this approach seeks to bring the world's forms of entertainment into the church in order to stimulate outreach and growth. Take the culture's forms of amusement, add society's latest trends, put a spiritual spin on it, and you will win the world. People should see little, if any, difference between the latest rock video—or a nightclub ensemble, or an off-Broadway production—and their church's worship service. Use the world to reach the world is their strategy.

Still others envision the church as being *driven by felt needs*. In other words, address the apparent, surface needs of people. Tell them how to find self-esteem, psychological significance, and personal success. Don't bore them with long discourses on the Bible. And, whatever you do, never mention the "s" word (sin) or the "h" word (hell). After all, who wants to hear what is negative?

Finally, there are those who, with good intentions, want the church to be *purpose driven*. Draft your church's vision statement, determine your objectives, define your long-term strategies, target a consumer group, develop a marketing plan, and you are in business. This Fortune 500 approach, lifted from the boardrooms of corporate America, says the church must be strategic, slick, and well run if it is to be successful.

Granted, there are elements in each of these approaches worth implementing. The church *should* be sensitive to personal needs, address the issues of the day, relate truth to people where they are, and be on-target with its mission. Who would argue with that? Any secular organization, from the local bank to the latest blue-chip company, wants to be people sensitive, market savvy, and influential.

The problem with all these approaches to the church, however, is that they lack depth. On the surface they sound fine. But, unfortunately, that is where they remain—on the surface.

Such radical shifts in the direction of the church are, I believe, the result of our diminished view of God. As our view of God has suffered, so have our ministries and lives. Rather than being focused upon the true God, we have become enamored with the world, a vantage point that easily accommodates our vision of a god made in our own image.

The sad result is this: Rather than seeking to become as much like heaven as they can be, churches are instead striving to become like the world. Rather than pursuing spirituality and substance, many have become enamored with style and size. The sizzle—not the steak—has become the main entrée. Gospel light is being replaced with gospel "lite," preaching with performance, exposition with entertainment, sound doctrine with sound checks, the upper room with the supper room, and the unfolding drama of redemption with—well, just plain drama.

Only when our vision of God is restored will our lives and ministries be put right. A high view of God leads us to see that the church is not a corporation, but a congregation; not a business, but a body; not a factory, but a family. In such a church, God works primarily not through hyped events, programs, entertainment, or even strategically designed plans per se, but through His Word and by His Spirit in the converted, changed lives of His people.

Sad to say, we have become preoccupied with everything but God. In the church, we are immersed in so many things—church growth, counseling, relationships, worship styles, leadership, time management, spiritual gifts, ministry, and the like. In their proper place these are all fine and good, but they should never become our obsession.

There can be only one subject on which we are most intently focused, and that is the person of God Himself. He is the one who made us in His image and redeemed our fallen souls; He is the one who indwells and fills our lives with good things. God—and God *alone*—must be the focus of our hearts.

Ultimately, a right vision of God must be the driving force behind the church. Only that can bring His glorious presence and all-sufficient power to bear on the lives of His people so that we can be what He desires us to be. We must unveil the truth about the sovereign God to unmask the fallacy of the user-friendly god. To that end I have written this book. I have written it in the firm conviction that *He* is the greatest truth and that how we view Him will affect how we see every other truth. May God bring a revival—a new reformation, if you will—in the knowledge of Him.

part one

~

THE EXPLOITATION

OF GOD

chapter one

ENCOUNTERING THE ALMIGHTY

The Contemplation of God

—

*People are starving for the greatness of God.
But most of them would not give this
diagnosis of their troubled lives. The
majesty of God is an unknown cure.*

JOHN PIPER

Has there ever been a time in your life when you came
face-to-face with God?

The real God, that is—the God who has revealed
Himself in Scripture as an awesome God we must know and worship. The God who defines Himself as love, but who also is a God
of wrath and judgment. The God who has no tolerance for sin, but
who also made it possible for people to have intimate fellowship
with Himself.

Have you ever come face-to-face with *this* God?

Can you remember a moment in your life when your preconceived notions of God were shattered, leaving you with a picture of
God as He really is? It is always a sobering encounter when God
reveals Himself to us—it is an experience that changes us forever.

MADE IN *OUR* IMAGE

I will never forget a time like that in my life when God, through the pages of Scripture, pulled back the veil and revealed Himself as far greater and grander than I had ever before imagined. It was a moment that changed my life immeasurably—and *forever!*

FACE-TO-FACE WITH GOD

There was a time when I thought I had God all figured out. That is not an uncommon thought for someone like I was at the time—a young, fledgling seminary student.

While I was studying at Dallas Theological Seminary, I knew just enough about God to be dangerous. I knew the gospel and understood some basic Bible doctrine. I could identify most of the characters in Scripture, as well as the high points of the story of redemption. I knew that God existed as one God but in three persons—the Father, the Son, and the Holy Spirit. I understood that He knew everything and could do anything. Furthermore, I knew He loved me and had a wonderful plan for my life.

These are all wonderful truths about God that I knew. So what more was there to learn about Him, right? The worst part of my spiritual ignorance at that time was that I had no idea how little I actually knew about God.

I really believed I had God all figured out, so I was content to cruise through my spiritual life, taking the path of least resistance, even as I prepared for the ministry. Everything in my life seemed predictable and routine. Although I was gaining much head knowledge about God, I pursued Him only halfheartedly and allowed myself to be beguiled by a world I had once forsaken. Using various worldly endeavors to put myself through seminary enticed me to dabble with the world once more.

Then, unexpectedly, I ventured upon a subject in God's Word

that confronted me, convicted me, and challenged me like no other truth I had ever encountered. It was a topic so vast, so towering, and so dominant that it overshadowed everything in my life. My heart was gripped as it had never been before. My soul was stunned as I studied it intensely for the very first time. The subject?

God.

AN EYE-OPENING EXPERIENCE

For the first time in my life, I began to see God for who He is. As I read my Bible, I observed truths about Him that didn't fit into my preconceived, self-fabricated notions. As I delved into the person of God, I saw truths about Him that seemed paradoxical.

I came face-to-face with certain aspects of God's character that I had never encountered before. Hard-core realities about His awesome holiness shook me to my core. Unexplored realms of His fierce wrath and irreversible judgments left me with a previously unknown sense of awe and fear. I wrestled with questions about His absolute sovereignty for which I had no simple answers. Here I was in seminary, preparing for ministry, and I found myself asking the question *Who is God?*

I had been a Christian since I was a child; but now I saw God as I had never seen Him before, and the effect on my life was nothing short of earthshaking. No longer did I have God figured out and neatly packaged in a small box. There was more to this God I served than I had previously imagined.

In reality, I was encountering what some have called "learned ignorance," meaning I was learning how truly ignorant I was about God—the most important of all subjects. That was the first of many steps toward my learning who He really is.

OBSESSED WITH GOD

Lying in bed at night, I contemplated the inscrutable truths of God's vast character, wrestling in my heart to comprehend Him. Driving in my car, I riveted my thoughts upon the infinite Deity. Sitting at the dinner table, I could think about nothing but God. I was literally obsessed with who He is. The larger He grew in my mind, the smaller I became.

Everything was being put into proper perspective, and I could no longer perceive God in humanlike terms. No longer could I think of Him as the God depicted in witty little slogans printed on Christian bumper stickers or in simple, trite terms stitched on sweatshirts. No longer could I think of God as one step above man, a glorified *us*.

Before, I mainly perceived His nearness; after, I stood face-to-face with His transcendence. Before, I focused mostly on His imminence; after, I was gripped by His immensity. Before, I marveled at His power; after, I struggled with His prerogative as the sovereign Lord of heaven and earth to exercise His power as He pleases, when He pleases, and toward whom He pleases.

My little mental box for God could no longer contain Him.

In this soul-churning time of inner reflection, I contemplated God's divine character and brooded over His perfect attributes. All the while, my life was being turned upside down. Although it was painful at the time, I was discovering firsthand that the subject of God Himself was the only truth large enough and captivating enough to reroute my drifting life. My life was being conquered by the sheer magnitude of who God is.

I am glad to say I have never been the same since.

Have you ever gone through a time like this? Have you ever had your thoughts of God expanded beyond the limits of your ability to think? Like an explorer scaling the thin air heights of Mount Everest, have you ever truly sought to climb the higher levels of knowing God?

A decision to do just that can change your life profoundly.

THE MOST IMPORTANT THING

The most important thing about you is who you believe God is. Tell me what comes into your mind when you think about God, and I will tell you everything else about your life. Everything about you flows from your understanding of who God is. What you think of God is the mainspring from which your entire being flows. Like the foundation of a house that supports the entire structure, your true, intimate knowledge of God is what upholds your life and gives it direction, purpose, and strength.

With keen insight, A. W. Tozer once observed that the gravest question before the church is always God Himself and that the most portentous fact about any man is not what he says or does at any given time, but what deep in his heart he conceives God to be like.

That kind of personal knowledge of God is the leading cause of which everything else in our lives is the resulting effect. Who we believe God is impacts every area of our lives—our attitudes, priorities, choices, and even our destiny. The true knowledge of God is so vast and overreaching that it is the only subject large enough, and powerful enough, to define and to determine every aspect of our lives.

There can be no subject more life changing than God, and there is no greater determinative factor in how you live your life than a true, right knowledge of who God really is.

The Determinative Factor

Nothing will change a person's life more than coming to know God in a personal, intimate way. That kind of relationship involves knowing God for who He really is—His character, His attributes, His personality. An accurate, high view of God leads to a wonderfully close relationship with our Lord that, in turn, leads to a life that is pleasing to Him.

But just as a true knowledge of God leads to right living before Him, a defective view of Him inevitably leads to faulty living. As surely as the lowering of the evening sun leads to physical darkness, a low view of God leads to base, insignificant living and even spiritual darkness. If our lives fall short, it is ultimately because our view of God falls short. Transcendent living arises from a surpassing knowledge of God. A high view of God will always lead to holy, passionate living.

Unquestionably, the knowledge of God is the only paradigm through which we can accurately perceive the world around us. How you view Him will dictate how you understand yourself, sin, salvation, society, eternity—*everything*. When your view of God is fuzzy, everything else is distorted. Conversely, a proper vision of God brings everything distinctly into focus.

Sadly, the right view of God—the view of Him we see in the Scriptures—is lacking in the lives of many believers today. Even many well-meaning Christians have fallen into the trap of espousing a low view of God. They have, most often unwittingly, allowed an inaccurate, nonbiblical picture of God to cloud and distort the perfect image of who He really is. Instead of worshiping and serving the one true God, they have taken to serving a god that is a mere shadow of the One who has revealed Himself in the Scriptures.

Let us take a look at that god for a moment.

THE "USER-FRIENDLY" GOD

A flawed view of God has emerged on the contemporary Christian scene. I call it a user-friendly picture of God. I use this pop-culture term because many present-day thoughts about God have been so trivialized that He appears humanlike with finite limitations. Instead of seeing man created in God's image, we are now configuring God into our image. Our perceptions of Him have become shamefully miniscule and man-centered.

As a result, our understanding of who God is has reached an all-time low, so much so that it is pulling everyone and everything else down with it. These demeaning pictures of God have ushered in a day of superficial living, shallow worship, and sterile evangelism. They are wreaking havoc on individual believers, as well as the corporate body of Christ in the church. Without a doubt, the church today is suffering from low views of the One who, in reality, is high and lifted up.

If we are to see a revival, true knowledge of God must be revived. Only a restoration in our understanding of who He is will be sufficient to turn the tide in our day. The subject of God is so great, and so powerful, that it is fully sufficient to revive our hearts, recharge our churches, and redirect our lives.

LIKE PRODUCES LIKE

There is a simple concept in biology that I will paraphrase: Like produces like. In other words, an offspring will always resemble its parents. Dogs give birth to dogs; horses give birth to horses; apes give birth to apes. You will never see a giraffe giving birth to a hippopotamus.

I use this simple illustration to demonstrate a principle that also applies to our spiritual lives. I believe that the user-friendly view of God has produced equally low levels of user-friendly Christian living, ministry, and worship. It is this user-friendly approach to God that is so debilitating to the church. Reducing God to the lowest possible common denominator results in a diminutive deity—a god-lite rather than the God who is light. The trivialization of God plagues contemporary Christianity with demeaning thoughts of God that are too shallow, too superficial, and too simplistic.

It is no wonder that we have so little impact on the world today. We have lost our vision of God. The only conclusion we can reach is that when we diminish our view of God, we decrease the dynamic of all things spiritual. I believe that what is needed these days more than anything else is a heaven-sent revival of the *true* knowledge of God.

As we rediscover who God truly is, our personal lives and churches will become the spiritual forces He desires. Only as we delve more deeply into God's Word and discover afresh His holy character and infinite attributes will we truly glorify His name and experience the fullness of all that He is. When that happens, we will be the salt and light in this dark world that the Lord Jesus Christ has called us to be. Like will produce *like!*

CHARTING OUR COURSE

In the course of this book, I will discuss the distortions of God I believe stunt our relationship with Him, consider how they are hindering our lives and churches today, and emphasize a proper understanding of who He is. In the same way a master detective would study the original to detect the counterfeit, we will examine the one, true God as revealed in Scripture in order to expose the user-friendly god that too many embrace. In the process of this investigation, we will consider the key attributes of God that must be firmly reestablished in our thinking: His holiness, sovereignty, wrath, love, and goodness. While there are other vital aspects of God's majestic character that we will contemplate, such as His omnipotence, omniscience, wisdom, truth, and immutability, we will consider them under those main headings.

After examining these divine characteristics, we will consider how they come together to constitute His glory. As the supreme revelation of all God is, His glory—the sum total of all His divine perfections—demands that we give Him glory, the only proper response due His name. Nowhere is this glory seen more clearly than in the death of His Son, Jesus Christ, on the cross. Thus, we will examine the unveiled glory of God in the cross as the greatest revelation of who God is.

In the final three chapters, we will consider the proper response to beholding the glory of God—knowing, fearing, and worshiping Him. Only when our view of God is right can we respond to God rightly. Based upon a correct view of who He is, we will seek to bring our own lives into alignment with Him and put everything else in its proper place. A right view of God is everything.

Do you want to have an encounter with the Almighty? Do you want to come to a deeper, fuller understanding of who He is? Do you want to have a high view of Him? I can assure you, we *cannot* have too high a view of God.

It is with that end in mind we begin.

chapter two

SPRAY PAINTING THE MASTERPIECE

The Distortion of God, Part 1

—

When a lie goes unanswered, it
becomes part of people's thinking.
D. JAMES KENNEDY

The Louvre in Paris, France, is home to some of the greatest masterpieces in the world. Originally built as a residence for the kings of France, this palace has been converted into a museum that houses stunning art treasures. Covering more than forty acres and containing some eight miles of galleries, it contains over a million works of fine art.

Among them is the renowned *Mona Lisa,* painted by Leonardo da Vinci, the legendary artist of the Italian Renaissance. This work of genius is a portrait of the wife of a Florentine merchant, Lisa del Giocondo, whose mysterious smile Leonardo made famous. To protect irreplaceable masterpieces like this, the security system at the Louvre is among the tightest and most sophisticated in the world.

Let me ask you to consider the unthinkable. Can you imagine the outrage that would ensue if vandals were to break into the Louvre and spray the *Mona Lisa* with paint? If that were to occur, the dastardly deed would be the lead story of the evening news as a crime of monumental proportions. Such a breach in security would create an international cry of outrage.

Having considered that, try to imagine a crime far more tragic. I can think of one.

FAR MORE TRAGIC

An offense greater by far than breaking into the Louvre and spray painting the *Mona Lisa* is the work of those who, whether intentionally or not, unlawfully enter the corridors of our hearts and despoil us of a true picture of God. The greatest sin anyone can commit is to distort the true knowledge of God. Vandalizing God's image—not with spray cans or permanent markers, but with loose thinking, partial truths, and bad theology—is at the center of every sin. Such sacrilege is a crime of the highest order.

Just as every measure of security is taken to guard the masterpieces that hang in museums around the world, even more so should we take every precaution to protect the greatest treasure of all—the image of God that hangs in our innermost being. We must carefully guard our thoughts of God because a distorted view of the Creator inevitably leads us, His creation, to live distorted lives.

A biblically trained eye can detect this desecration of the divine likeness. A demeaned view of the one true God is the result of a pattern of compromise—from watered-down sermons presenting a low view of God to the trendy music of Christian performers who crossover to secular markets but forget to carry the Cross with them. The original *Master*piece has been marred; the counterfeits are on sale as cheap substitutes.

Worse, people are buying this user-friendly image of God.

MISUNDERSTANDING GOD

I believe that well-meaning Christians—people truly interested in seeing others brought into the kingdom—often promote these distortions of God. They are a product more of carelessness than guile. Trying to make the faith more user-friendly, they present a god who loves and forgives, but never judges or punishes: a god who is compassionate and patient, but not completely holy; and a god who gave all He had to us in the form of His Son, Jesus Christ, but expects nothing in return, not even a change in our lives.

These simplistic, humanlike views of God are what I call a user-friendly approach to God. Popular in the computer industry, the term describes something that is very difficult to understand, such as computer software or hardware, but that has been made so simple that anyone can use it. All difficulty and intimidation are removed. Otherwise inaccessible to the masses, using a computer is now so easy that even the uneducated can do it.

As it relates to deity, that's what a user-friendly god means. It is the principle of the lowest common denominator. God has been so dumbed down that all fear and reverence are removed for those who wish to approach Him. Stripped of His unspeakable majesty, He is reduced to the lowest possible level, where anyone can access and use Him.

This user-friendly god, however, is the product of man's own sinful imagination—a god of our own making. The true God has been recast in the mold of worldly interests, hammered upon the anvil of our own selfish desires, and plated with the cheap tinsel of pragmatic pursuits. In no way resembling the holy, sovereign God of heaven and earth, He has become, in reality, a god made in *our* own image.

A. W. Tozer once made an insightful observation about this

trend of aberrant thinking. He said that as the twentieth century progressed, the Christian conception of God became so decadent as to be utterly beneath the dignity of the Most High God and that, for professed believers, it actually constituted something amounting to a moral calamity.

What Tozer realized was that secular influences had minimized even the church's view of God.

WHO CREATED WHOM?

Voltaire once said, "God created man in His own image, and man has returned the favor." The eighteenth-century French philosopher was belittling the notion that there was one true God who had uniquely created mankind in His own likeness. Like other agnostics before and since, Voltaire believed that man creates the notion of God in the laboratory of his own genius, casting a deity in his own image with finite limitations and humanlike qualities. Like a person looking in a mirror and then forming his thoughts about himself based on what he sees, so man creates God in his own likeness by looking inward, not upward. This god is the result of reflection, not revelation.

Regrettably, this kind of idolatrous thinking is common, not only among agnostics like Voltaire who reject the Bible, but also among professing believers who neglect the clear teaching of Scripture. Left to our own fallen imaginations, we tend to perceive the infinite God in light of our finite limitations. The by-product of vain rationalizations about God will always find us reducing Him to a diminutive deity, one made in *our* own image, as we project our personal attitudes and desires on Him.

The Heart of the Matter

Herein lies the problem. Rather than allowing our thoughts about God to rise from Scripture, we let our own base, man-centered ideas govern how we view Him. All too often, we confine God to the small box of our finite minds—and our minds are incredibly small! The Bible, however, directs us to look beyond our limited human understanding and instead think lofty, exalted, truly worthy thoughts of God based on His Word.

Whenever we minimize God's Word, playing fast and loose with its truths, we worship the god of our imagination instead of the true God of Scripture. Along these lines, Isaiah laments:

> "For My thoughts are not your thoughts,
> Nor are your ways My ways," says the LORD.
> "For as the heavens are higher than the earth,
> So are My ways higher than your ways,
> And My thoughts than your thoughts."
>
> ISAIAH 55:8–9, NKJV

This means that left to our own reasoning, we will never understand who God truly is. It is critical that our ideas of God—the *most* important thing about us—correspond to who He has revealed Himself to be in Scripture.

What are some of the images of God we have created? What does the user-friendly god look like? What are some of the humanistic molds into which people cast God? What are some of the man-centered caricatures that many people today are substituting for the true knowledge of God? Read on!

God in Our Image

I would like to consider some of these false images of God by using several analogies to show how we have made God in *our* own image. The following are common misconceptions about who God is that have reduced Him to user-friendly status. While most of them contain some element of truth, they are nonetheless distortions of the true nature of God.

A Celestial Santa Claus

One of the earliest memories many children have is anticipating the arrival of Santa Claus on Christmas Eve. Santa looms larger than life in the minds of many youngsters. Jolly ol' Saint Nick seems almost godlike. He is perceived to be omniscient, omnipresent, and omnipotent, to say nothing of all-giving, all-loving, and all-wise.

Santa lives at the North Pole surrounded by his helpers. He keeps a list, checks it twice, and finds out who is naughty and nice. Then once a year he visits everyone's house around the globe, freely bestowing good gifts from above and making everyone happy. This benevolent bearer of bountiful gifts makes no demands on anyone's life. He is always aware of what everyone wants and travels from house to house to dispense his treasures, only to reappear the following year with another rewarding visit.

It is not stretching the point to say that many people have the same kind of image of God: He exists simply to meet needs in their lives and requires nothing in return except a little good behavior now and then. Like Santa Claus, God exists to provide but never to discipline or punish.

Is this how God should be perceived? Certainly not! Such a lowly perception of Him degrades His holy nature and righteous being. While God *does* bestow good gifts on us, He also withholds, convicts, disciplines, rebukes, and challenges. Our mistake is to forget that although He is a giving God, He is also a consuming fire who dwells in blazing, unapproachable light that no man can access through his own goodness. Yes, God wants to provide and give us good things, but this view of Him is way out of balance.

A DIVINE COPILOT

There is another distortion of God prevalent in our midst today: viewing Him as a divine copilot.

Every time I step on an airplane, I see one. He is positioned at the front door of the plane, smiling and welcoming everyone coming on board. His job is to be on standby—ready to step in and help should an unexpected emergency demand it. While the pilot bears the major responsibility for flying the plane, the copilot is there to grab the controls when needed to help steer the plane in the right direction, steady the plane in times of turbulence, and keep an observant eye on the instrument panel. Should anything go wrong, he comforts the passengers over the loudspeakers. However, once the emergency is over, he returns control to the pilot. He is always *at* the controls but never totally *in* control.

Sadly, that is precisely how the user-friendly god is perceived. I know because I read it on bumper stickers all the time. The message is plain as day: "Jesus Is My Copilot." How convenient it is to have a subordinate sovereign—able to drive, but only at our discretion! Reduced to a secondary, supportive role, the Lord is always there, watching and awaiting our call in times of crisis. But in the interim He does little. Occasionally, He checks our instrument panels, ready to step in if needed, or comforts us when something goes wrong; but for the most part He is on standby. His will is always subordinate to ours.

Under this scheme, who is the pilot? Unfortunately, *we* are. Remaining in control, *we* sit in the pilot's seat, bearing the main responsibility of keeping our lives moving in the right direction. He is always there like a loyal assistant, ready and willing to give His opinion, but not acting until asked.

Is this how God is to be perceived? Is He our copilot, ready to step in only when we need Him? Or is He something more? Is not Jesus Christ to be our Lord as well as Savior? Does He not want to take complete control of our lives, making *us* the subordinates? Clearly, we are not to view God as our divine copilot.

A HEAVENLY REPAIR MAN

Unfortunately, there is a third distortion of God: seeing Him as a heavenly repairman.

There is a man in our church named Neal, a good man who can fix anything and who is always willing to lend a hand. I happen to know this because he offers his services to help around our house. This is a great asset to me because I cannot repair a thing. But if Neal, a retired school maintenance man, cannot fix it, no one can.

Neal often reminds us that he is only a phone call away. Even better, because he is a benevolent person, he does not charge us for his services. Many times we have sent in a distress call to him when something has stopped working at our home. True to his offer, he comes immediately and fixes whatever is broken. Neal is so helpful that he has surprised us by doing a home improvement project without our even asking. We have yet to find something he cannot fix.

Unfortunately, many people view God as a benevolent jack-of-all-trades who can fix anything. They see His goodness merely in a problem-solving capacity. They see Him as an on-duty repairman, always ready to fix whatever has broken in their lives. While we all know God can solve any problem and is always there when we need Him, this view of God as a repairman robs Him of His true goodness.

To view God merely as Mr. Fix-It makes Him worthless to us when we do not need repairs in our lives. What this view of God implies is that He's great when we are in a fix, but unnecessary when everything is going well.

The truth is that God is our Redeemer, a fountain of goodness that we draw from in prosperity as well as in adversity. He is not a divine repairman we can call in a crunch. We need God's goodness at *all* times, not only when something is broken in our lives, but also when everything appears to be running smoothly.

The Bible says,

> For the LORD is good,
> For His lovingkindness is everlasting.
> JEREMIAH 33:11

Because His goodness is everlasting, it is constant—forever the same in all situations of life.

A GALACTIC GRANDFATHER

A fourth regrettable distortion of God is regarding him as a galactic grandfather.

Most grandfathers seem to be cut out of the same mold—abundant in love and affection, yet lacking in discipline. Wise old men who exude serenity and devotion, they spend most of their time and effort spoiling their grandchildren. Their admonitions go unheeded; their threats are just that—threats; and in the end, "Grandpa" can be won with a shed tear or a gentle hug on his leg.

As long as their grandchildren talk to them and acknowledge their love, grandfathers are satisfied. They enjoy nothing more than their grandchildren's company; and even when the grandkids misbehave, grandfathers just smile and reaffirm their love. They do not get angry; their feelings are never hurt; and they certainly do not discipline. Their days of dealing with wrongdoing are long past. The children can do whatever they want around them without fear. It seems as if their sole reason for existence is to be taken advantage of.

The imagery is clear. Many perceive God exactly like a galactic grandfather. They see Him as a doting deity who merely wants to love us all over, never showing a trace of displeasure or discipline. Simply tell Him what is happening; try to do more good than bad; and He will understand. Sure, they know God talks about sin, but they have seemingly gone unpunished for so long that they think this senile sovereign no longer means what He says. They rush headlong into sin because they can always ask forgiveness later. After all, it is easier to get forgiveness than permission.

But this is certainly not what God is like! While He is loving and forgiving, He is also a God of wrath and justice. He has saved us not to spoil us, but to sanctify us. He is not our "grandpa," but our holy Father.

A UNIVERSAL UTILITARIAN

Emerging from a different crowd is another falsely fabricated view of God, that of the universal utilitarian. This disfiguration of God presents Him as a dispassionate king who rules His creation with an iron fist. Like a war commander who doesn't care for the well-being of his soldiers, God is distant, detached, and preoccupied.

This view of God is based on the reasoning that He is powerful enough to stop such tragedies as natural disasters, sinister rulers, and bloody wars but does not; therefore, He must not be a good God. People who reason this way view God as nothing more than a utilitarian who stoically orchestrates events to His appointed end, but not for our good.

However, this is not who God is. Our thoughts of Him must be biblical; and as we view God through the lens of Scripture, we can know that He is good in all His ways and that He greatly cares for us (Luke 18:19).

A CLEVER MAGICIAN

There is yet one more distortion of God affecting our lives today—depicting Him as a clever magician.

We have all seen an awe-inspiring illusionist on television, or perhaps in person. He does the seemingly impossible—defies natural laws, causes people to disappear, pulls animals out of hats, and saws attendants in two. It is not hard to watch the illusionist because he is so entertaining. His magic acts, wizardry, and apparent supernatural powers mesmerize his spellbound audience.

The illusionist is really more of a showman than anything else. He will do whatever it takes to pack people into the auditorium. A boring show is a bad show. The goal is to keep the performance spectacular and the people coming, however you get them there. Bigger is almost always better.

Unfortunately, some Christians think of God as just such an illusionist. They assume He must always work through signs, miracles, and wonders. In fact, if there is no visible manifestation of power, they conclude God must really be uninvolved. "Slaying in the spirit," "words of knowledge," "levitation"—all these things are presumed to be necessary evidences of God's presence.

But is this God? Is this how He works in our lives? Is He to be perceived in this way? Or, is this merely a god made in our own image, the result of our own fanciful desires?

HAS ANYONE SEEN GOD LATELY?

All these misconceptions about God grossly malign the proper knowledge of who He truly is. Although all contain some elements of truth—often buried under the untruths—they do more harm than good. As J. I. Packer once lamented, "When half the truth becomes the whole truth, the result is no truth." Like the proverbial clock that does not run but is correct twice a day, these gross misrepresentations of God's character are more wrong than right; and they obscure the true glory of the One who is infinite, eternal, and beyond our comprehension.

To think of God in any way other than how He has disclosed Himself in the full counsel of Scripture is to be guilty of the sin of idolatry. Although idolatry manifests itself in many different ways, it is nothing more than having a wrong perception of God and acting as if it were true.

Our lives always put into action our thoughts of God. Therefore, we must think rightly about Him if our lives are to be right. And the only way to think rightly about Him is to look carefully into His Word and submit to its truth. God must reveal from above the truth about Himself; we cannot conjure worthy thoughts about Him from our own imaginations.

As you continue through the pages of this book, I pray that the Lord will lead you to a high and holy view of Himself.

chapter three

REDUCING THE IRREDUCIBLE

The Distortion of God, Part 2

*Idolatry is the greatest insult
the creature can offer the Creator.*
CHARLES HADDON SPURGEON

Augustine, the great thinker and theologian of yesteryear, was once walking along an ocean beach greatly perplexed by the incomprehensible truth of the Trinity. Try as he might, he could not grasp the vast truth of the triune nature of God. Because he could not fully understand it, he was tempted to reject it.

Augustine continued to walk along the shoreline until he came upon a little boy playing on the beach. As he watched the child, he saw him run to the ocean with a seashell, fill it with water, and then return to pour it into a small hole he had dug in the sand.

"What are you doing, my little man?" asked Augustine.

"Oh," replied the boy, "I am trying to put the ocean into this hole."

Augustine smiled at the little boy's faith in the face of the impossibility of such a task. Then it suddenly struck him that, when it came to God, he was guilty of exactly the same thing. "That is what I am trying to do with God," the saint later confessed. "I see it now. Standing on the shores of time, I am trying to get into this little finite mind things which are infinite."

THE REDUCTION OF GOD

We are all guilty of trying to do what Augustine was tempted to do. In one way or another, we all attempt to reduce God to humanlike dimensions based on what we can logically understand by our limited thinking. We are all tempted to think of Him on our level. But such self-conceived perceptions are always disastrous. They signal our departure from the true knowledge of God and lead to idolatry.

The diminishing of God is nothing new. It has occurred throughout human history since the Creation. Beginning in the Garden of Eden and continuing to the present, the distortion of God's glory occurs all around us, leaving a trail of damaged faith, dishonorable worship, disoriented lives, and ineffective ministry in its wake. Like a mind-altering drug that inhibits one's ability to function properly, a warped view of God destroys the spiritual compass of one's soul.

With God-inspired wisdom, Solomon wrote, "Where there is no vision, the people are unrestrained" (Proverbs 29:18). The word *vision* refers to the divine revelation recorded in His Word through which God made known to us His perfect, holy character. The vision of Scripture is primarily a vision of God Himself, brought into focus before the watching eyes of the reader. Without the proper vision of God to which Solomon referred, we too would self-destruct.

With this in mind, let us begin our biblical survey of the danger of distorting God's glory. In this chapter, I want to trace the unfolding stages of this destructive, lethal sin through the pages of Scripture. Let us begin with where it all started: in the Garden.

IN THE BEGINNING...

When God created the world, it was without blemish or defect. In fact, after each day of Creation, God could only conclude that it was "good." Most of all, God's relationship with Adam and Eve, the crown of His creation, was good. As God walked with them in the Garden, their knowledge of Him was true, pure, and genuine. They knew God for who He is.

But that was before sin entered the world. At the very outset of human history, the initial sin was a deadly departure from the true knowledge of God. In the Garden of Eden, Satan slithered onto the stage of human history and spoke those now-infamous words to Eve: "Indeed, has God said, 'You shall not eat from any tree of the garden?'" (Genesis 3:1). With that question—in reality, a scandalous statement concerning the very person of God—the devil intentionally spray painted graffiti on Eve's picture of God and defaced God's holy character.

Before the Fall, God had revealed Himself fully to this first couple. First, He had revealed that He is absolutely holy. The One who makes a distinction between good and evil prohibited them from eating from the tree of the knowledge of good and evil. He revealed Himself to be a loving God who had joyfully provided for man by putting him in a beautiful paradise to enjoy. He revealed Himself to be righteous, establishing a just penalty—death—for disobeying Him and partaking of the forbidden fruit. He revealed Himself to be sovereign, which means that He possesses power over life and death itself and that He decrees the eternal destinies of men and women. In all this, God revealed Himself as One who wanted Adam and Eve to fellowship with Him in an intimate, personal relationship.

But now with this one distortion, the devil perverted Eve's thinking about God, slipped past her guard, and altered her mental picture of Him. In essence, the evil one said, "You have got God all wrong! You need to see Him in a different light. He is holding out on you. If God were good, He would let you eat of this tree."

FORBIDDEN THOUGHTS OF GOD

Without Eve's understanding what was happening, Satan staged a mental break-in and vandalized her picture of God. Her image of deity was completely destroyed, and soon her life would be as well. Before the first couple ate of the forbidden fruit, Eve had entertained forbidden thoughts about God. It was her wrong view of Him that led to their sinful choice. The original sin was conceived when their understanding of God was confused, compromised, and finally, corrupted. Having accomplished this, the devil had polluted the most cherished treasure of God's prized Creation. He had distorted their picture of God.

Soon after her own deception, Eve got her husband to eat the fruit. Consequently, the entire human race was thrown into cosmic rebellion against God, into a state of enmity with Him from which—but for God's redemptive grace—we could never recover. It was the darkening of Eve's understanding of who God is that led to her sin and to every subsequent transgression in human history. No longer perceiving Him to be holy, she falsely pictured God and thus blurred the distinctions between good and evil. No longer seeing God as loving, she wrongly assumed He was withholding His goodness. No longer seeing Him as righteous, she actually believed God would not punish sin. Once these aberrations occurred in her thinking about God, the result was inevitable—she disobeyed Him.

Soon thereafter, God placed a judicial curse upon all His Creation because of this breach of His Word. Women would bear children in pain; Satan would slither on the ground; man would work by the sweat of his brow (Genesis 3:14–19)—all because of Adam's original sin, an act of disobedience that resulted from Eve's wrong view of God. That is how serious it is to misunderstand God. In one way or another, all man's subsequent woes can be traced back to a distorted view of deity.

I believe this beguilement is taking place all around us today. Satan has crept undetected into our lives and churches, whispering in our ears time and again, "Has God indeed said?" and causing us to question His holiness, love, sovereignty, and righteousness. In so many ways we have allowed the devil to distort our view of God, and that has led us down a path of poor choices, starting with the one to make God in our image.

As we see in Scripture, the devil continued to distort the true picture of God after the Garden of Eden.

THE SECOND COMMANDMENT

In the generations after the first couple's reimaging of God, man's perceptions of Him were further assailed by the influences of false religions and idolatry, which were literally perfected to an art form. That is why when God gave the Ten Commandments, first and foremost He established what was *most* important to us—the true knowledge of Himself.

It is no coincidence that the revered law of Moses begins with the imperative to protect our thoughts of God and to keep them worthy of Him. Revealing His holy character, God commanded, "You shall have no other gods before Me. You shall not make for yourself an idol, or any likeness of what is in heaven above or on the earth beneath or in the water under the earth" (Exodus 20:3–4).

In these first two commandments, God revealed what is most important to us; namely, our supreme commitment to the true knowledge of who He is. They are like interconnecting links in an unbreakable chain. In the first commandment, God prohibits us from worshiping other gods; in the second, He forbids us to distort the true picture of God by any physical or mental representations of Him.

Any man-made likeness of God inevitably falls short of His infinite perfection, and so distorts His glorious being. Anything man makes to represent God, whether it is an inanimate idol or other visual representation of deity, will always defile the true knowledge of God. A departure from these commandments—truly the pivotal, watershed commandments—only leads down the destructive path of dishonoring God.

THE HEART OF THE MATTER

This sin of creating man-made likenesses of God is not limited to making physical idols or representations of Him. It also includes the ones we can so easily and sometimes unknowingly set up in our hearts and minds. We can violate the second commandment not only with our hands, but worse, with our *hearts* and *minds*.

This is true with each of the Ten Commandments. God tells us through the Scriptures that the inner life—the condition of our hearts—is more important than the outer life. The Bible tells us:

> Watch over your heart with all diligence,
> For from it flow the springs of life.
> PROVERBS 4:23

The heart is most important because it controls everything about us.

In the Sermon on the Mount, Jesus stated that each of the Ten

Commandments was meant to be a matter of our hearts (Matthew 5:21–30). The Lord taught that murder can be committed not only by taking another life, but also by hating another person (vv. 21–24). Likewise, He pointed out that adultery can be committed not only through unlawful overt sexual activity, but also within one's own heart (vv. 27–30).

In similar fashion, while the second commandment directly prohibits fabricating a physical idol with one's hands, it also prohibits crafting unworthy thoughts of God in our hearts and minds. The former implies the latter, and the external implies the internal. Therefore, whenever we think untrue thoughts of God, whenever we allow unscriptural pictures of God to hang in our hearts, we forge idols on the anvils of our minds, resulting in demeaning caricatures of the divine.

Low thoughts of God are as blasphemous as wooden, man-made idols. They are a deadly poison to our faith and destroy our true knowledge of God. The distorting of true deity is a serious sin, so serious in the Old Testament economy that it brought God's curse (Deuteronomy 27:15).

A "NEW" IDOLATRY

This sin is not one that is limited to Old Testament times. In fact, I believe we see the second commandment violated in many ways today. As God's people, it is our job to safeguard the true knowledge of Him; but in many ways we have let down our guard and allowed wrong views of God to be hung in the corridors of our minds. Instead of protecting our hearts and minds, we have allowed every influence imaginable to alter our picture of God, resulting in distorted, dishonoring images of Him. This has had a devastating effect on the church today.

Should we be surprised that Scripture admonishes us to guard our hearts and minds? I think not. Solomon, the wisest man who ever lived, warned us in Proverbs 4:23 to diligently guard our hearts and minds because in doing so we guard our very lives. From them our entire life flows. And the key to keeping our minds right is having the right knowledge of God (2 Corinthians 10:5).

Turn on most modern-day Christian television broadcasts or listen to much of contemporary Christian music, and you will see that the theological safeguards of the picture of the true character of God have been discarded. One mindless chorus goes so far as to celebrate Jesus as "the salt on my Frito," a staggering trivialization of the Lord Jesus Christ.

With godly passion, we must recognize that the full force of these first two commandments is still in effect today and must determine to direct our lives to the worship of the one true God.

THE GOLDEN CALF

As God's drama in Scripture continues, we see Him continuing to protect the revelation of who He is. When Moses descended Mount Sinai after receiving the Ten Commandments, he rejoined the people camped below, understanding as never before the supreme importance of guarding the true knowledge of God. After all, Moses had just had a personal encounter with almighty God!

Moses knew that no false gods or any distorted representations of the true God could be tolerated. In one way or another, each commandment God gave Moses was a manifestation of His holy character, thus requiring the allegiance and obedience of His people to keep His Word and to guard His glory.

Unfortunately, even before Moses came down from the mountain, the people of Israel were making themselves a god in their own image. The people said to Aaron, "Come, make us a god who will go before us" (Exodus 32:1). Aaron gave in to the people, told them to pool their gold, and "fashioned it with a graving tool, and made it into a molten calf" (v. 4). When the people saw the newly crafted idol, they exclaimed, "This is your god!" (v. 4). Aaron then built an altar and called for a feast. The next day, the people made offerings and sacrifices to the idol, worshiping it in a way that was to be reserved for the one true God. Despite the fact that God had delivered them from Egyptian bondage and despite the fact that He had performed so many miracles on their behalf, not the least of which was His parting of the Red Sea to deliver them from Pharaoh's army, they still clamored for this idol, a god of their own making.

When Moses descended the mountain and entered camp, he was not prepared for what he saw. God's people, instead of worshiping the true God, were committing base idolatry, bowing down before a god made by their own hands. When Moses saw them worshiping the golden calf, he threw the Ten Commandments to the ground, took the calf, burned it, ground it to powder, scattered it over the water, and made the people drink it. The next day Moses said to them, "You yourselves have committed a great sin" (v. 30).

A great sin? In reality, they had committed the *greatest* sin, the desecration of the true knowledge of God. God's people could have performed no greater evil than constructing this false deity and substituting it for the true God. A careful reading ahead in the Scripture reveals how God punished those who took part in the idolatry, a reminder of the seriousness of making another god in our own image.

All these thousands of years later this sin continues. Golden calves are still being erected today—not literally made with gold and crafted in the form of an animal, but far worse, being cast in the minds of people who have strayed from the true knowledge of God.

Whenever people turn away from the truth of God's Word, they invent a caricature of the true God and worship at the shrine of their own futile imagination. Making our own god is the *grossest* sin of all.

PURGING THE LAND

Following Moses' death, Joshua became his successor; and God commissioned him to lead His people into the Promised Land (Joshua 1:1–9). As Joshua led them into this new land, God commanded them to exterminate His enemies—the Ammonites, Hittites, Perizzites, Cananites, Hivites, and Jebusites. Why would God make such a hard request? What could these people possibly have done that was so serious that God required the death of men, women, children, and even babies?

Quite simply, the reason was that these pagan tribes worshiped false gods, and in so doing, they corrupted the authentic knowledge of God. All idolaters—men, women, and children—were to be killed to purge the land from their false gods. Although the remedy was severe, a wrong view of God is *that* serious.

As God commanded, Joshua led Israel to Jericho where "they utterly destroyed everything in the city, both man and woman, young and old, and ox and sheep and donkey, with the edge of the sword" (Joshua 6:21). They did so with a holy zeal to remove the false knowledge of false, man-made gods and to restore a correct understanding of the true God.

Anything that threatened the true knowledge of God was to be dealt with severely because it was an affront to His glory. Because of their idolatry, even their animals—oxen, sheep, and donkeys—were to be killed. Every trace of their blasphemous sin was to be obliterated. Not one trace of their misrepresentation of God was to remain.

With righteous passion, we too should champion the true

knowledge of God. Although we are no longer under the old covenant, an economy of God that required death for such an offense, we should nevertheless deal with misperceptions of God in our own hearts and put to death any idolatrous thoughts that misrepresent Him.

REMOVING FALSE ALTARS

Unfortunately, Joshua failed to eradicate all the heathen tribes from the Promised Land as God had commanded. Instead, he left pockets of false religions scattered throughout the land. The consequences of Joshua's failure were profound.

As time passed, the idolatrous influences grew exponentially; and combined with the pagan influences of the surrounding nations, these distortions of God plagued the land of Israel. Some of the names of these false gods were Adrammelech, Anamnelech, Ashima, Ashtoreth, Baal, Baal-beith, Baalzebub, Bel, Chemosh, Chiun, Dagon, Huzzab, Molech, Merodach, Nergal, Nebo, Nibhaz, Nisroch, Queen of heaven, Rimmon, Succothbenoth, and Tammuz. The evil was legion.

Although these evil influences persisted, God periodically sent revivals to His people. During these times of spiritual awakening, the people destroyed the altars of idols and restored the true knowledge of God. In one way or another, every revival was a rebirth of the proper understanding of who God is.

One such spiritual awakening took place under King Asa, a noble and good king of Judah, of whom it was written, "Asa did good and right in the sight of the LORD his God, for he removed the foreign altars and high places, tore down the sacred pillars, cut down the Asherim" (2 Chronicles 14:2–3). "High places" were elevated altars upon which sacrifices were made to pagan gods.

Surrounding these high places were sacred pillars, a part of the architecture of these demonic temples. Within these houses of worship were the Asherim, which caricatured the sexual orgies that accompanied their false religion. The writer of this inspired record would have us see the urgency of removing false gods from the land and destroying the items used in pagan worship.

All such idolatry *had* to be removed if a spiritual revival were to come. As you can imagine, these ancient places of worship were immoral as well as idolatrous. But the greatest evil was the perversion of the people's picture of who God is and their erecting a representation of a god of their own making. With a heart jealous for God's glory, Asa courageously ordered the removal of all such blasphemous offenses to the living God. Revival could not come until wrong views of God were removed.

As it was in Asa's day, so it is in ours. In much of the church today, spiritual idolatry, the distortion of who God is, is leading to immorality—whether in the form of physical or spiritual adultery. Before a true, heaven-sent revival can take place, all wrong views of God must be removed. A spiritual awakening will never come where there are low views of God. If we are to see revival in our day, we must first remove our unworthy thoughts of God and replace them with the true knowledge of God.

THE GREATEST SIN

Any departure from the true knowledge of God will always result in idolatry, false religion, and ruin. In Romans 1:18, the apostle Paul makes this clear: "For the wrath of God is revealed from heaven against all ungodliness and unrighteousness of men, who suppress the truth in unrighteousness."

Paul continues:

Because that which is known about
God is evident within them;
for God made it evident to them.
For since the creation of the world
His invisible attributes, His eternal power
and divine nature, have been clearly seen,
being understood through what has been made,
so that they are without excuse.

ROMANS 1:19–20

Knowledge about God is universal, available to all people, and unmistakably known by all.

God has planted in every person the true witness of who He is. All creation explicitly declares who He is. As Creator, He is revealed as sovereign, omnipotent, omnipresent, all-wise, and good, so that every person is without excuse.

Yet, although all people have access to the true knowledge of God through creation, conscience, and especially, God's Word, they choose to reject the truth about God in order to keep their sin. Paul writes: "For even though they knew God, they did not honor Him as God, or give thanks; but they became futile in their speculations, and their foolish heart was darkened" (v. 21). Refusing light increases darkness. Suppressing the true knowledge of God and failing to glorify Him result, Paul says, in spiritual ignorance of God.

When people reject the truth of God, they construct their own thoughts about Him; and the result is a man-made idol. "Professing to be wise, they became fools, and exchanged the glory of the incorruptible God for an image in the form of corruptible man and of birds and four-footed animals and crawling creatures" (vv. 22–23). Sound familiar? The worship of the true God is replaced with the worship of idols, gods made in our own image.

THE POINT OF NO RETURN

This downward spiral hits the point of no return. If people will not receive the truth about who God is, He will give them over to a deviant lifestyle and further distortions of who He is. Paul concludes, "Therefore God gave them over in the lusts of their hearts to impurity, that their bodies might be dishonored among them. For they exchanged the truth of God for a lie, and worshiped and served the creature rather than the Creator, who is blessed forever. Amen" (vv. 24–25).

This *is* the deadly game of distorting God. Whenever one rejects the true knowledge of God, it inevitably leads to creating a man-made god to worship. Such idolatry is the result of refusing the truth about God, which has been made known to all men everywhere. Once an individual erects a false god, God will give that person over to all sorts of other lies, defiled living, and if there is no repentance, eternal destruction.

What is the first step on this downward descent? Exchanging the truth about God for a lie. This is the fork in the road for all men. One path leads to heaven, the other down into the pit of destruction.

Therefore, we must guard the true knowledge of God with all our might. We must maintain a high view of God, uninfluenced by humanlike limitations and exalted in its presentation of His greatness.

LET ME SEE THEE!

I began this chapter by talking about Augustine, one of the greatest theologians of the church age. Throughout his life, he quested to know the infinite God in deeper ways.

It is reported that on one occasion, Augustine offered a daring prayer reflecting his passion to know the inscrutable God who dwells in unapproachable light. In his prayer, he pleaded with God, "Lord, hast Thou declared that no man shall see Thy face and live? Then let me die that I may see Thee."

This must be the one holy passion of our lives as well. We, too, must be in a relentless pursuit of the true knowledge of God, carefully avoiding the deadly sin of shrinking the infinite into the finite.

May our prayer be "Let me see *Thee!*"

part two

⁓

THE ESSENCE

OF GOD

chapter four

SO, WHO REALLY *IS* GOD?

The Person of God

---

*Bring me a worm that can
comprehend a man, and then
I will show you a man that can
comprehend the triune God!*

JOHN WESLEY

A father watched his young son, who was sprawled out on the floor of his bedroom, drawing a picture. Intensely focused, the child was fully engrossed in his work of art. Crayons had been scattered everywhere. Unfinished sketches had been wadded up and cast aside.

Not wanting to break the child's concentration, the father gently inquired, "Say, son, what are you drawing?"

Without even pausing to look up, the small boy replied, "God."

Somewhat taken back, his father said, "Well, no one knows what God looks like."

Confidently gazing at his masterpiece, the boy replied, "They will when I'm finished."

Much like this boy, we all have a picture of God in our minds. And our picture of God is critically important to who we are. In fact, as previously noted, our picture of God is *the* most important thing about us.

WHAT'S YOUR PICTURE OF GOD?

Too often, we allow our surroundings and imagination, instead of Scripture, to govern our thoughts about who God is. We often project our self-limitations on to our picture of Him, resulting in a god made in our own image. This is the curse of the user-friendly god—namely, low views of Him who is high and lifted up, finite views of Him who is infinite and beyond our comprehension.

A classic example of this reimaging of God occurred in Israel's past when God said through the psalmist, "You thought that I was just like you" (Psalm 50:21). The sin for which God rebuked His people was reducing Him to their level. Although they were faithfully going through the outward motions of worship—bringing their sacrifices, giving their offerings, and teaching the Scripture (vv. 8–11, 16)—their hearts were woefully wrong. What was causing them to miss the mark? Their unworthy thoughts of God. Their picture of God was totally wrong. Conversely, if they had revived their knowledge of God, they would have restored their own true worship and walk before Him.

The people of Israel should have been asking themselves the same questions we should ask today. Namely, who really *is* God? How *should* we think of Him? What *is* He like? What *is* His nature? What *should* be our picture of God?

WHO IS GOD?

Many people, consciously or unconsciously, make up their own definition of who God is. We must be sure we are talking about the

God of Scripture when we address the question, "Who is God?" It would take a large book to define God, and even then it would be incomplete.

Our definition of God should not be left up to our own imaginations; it must be determined from the pages of the Bible. When it comes to defining who God is, individual speculation is no more valid than a roll of the dice. The God we are talking about is the Creator of the universe, the original being, the sovereign ruler of all that is. He is the sole judge of all that is true and false, right and wrong, good and bad. He is the One who communicates to humankind generally in nature and specifically through the words of the Bible.

The fourth question in the Westminster Shorter Catechism, a teaching curriculum used in many Presbyterian churches, is "What is God?" The answer is: "God is a Spirit, infinite, eternal, and unchangeable in His being, wisdom, power, holiness, justice, goodness, and truth." The late theologian Charles Hodges described this statement as "probably the best definition of God ever penned by man."

FRAMING THE DIVINE PICTURE

Questions about the person of God are not easily answered. However, we may be confident that the Bible, when rightly understood, provides us with clear answers, accurately framing our picture of the true God. My purpose is to bring into focus a proper picture of God.

We will begin by considering what Bible teachers call the essence of God, or the inner reality of who and what He is. The divine essence is that which underlies all outward manifestations of His being. It is the divine substance underlying His perfect being to which His attributes and character adhere.

Broadly speaking, the Bible teaches that God is spirit, invisible, infinite, self-existent, self-sufficient, and eternal while possessing all the components of personality—mind, emotion, and will. All these aspects describe the substance of God's character and define who He is. If our picture of God is to be accurate, then we must be clear in our understanding of these truths. Let us consider each of these aspects of the divine nature.

GOD IS SPIRIT

First, the Bible teaches that God is spirit. This means that He is not a material being. He is not tangible or physical. Rather, He is a spiritual being without a physical body. Clarifying this point, Jesus said, "God is spirit" (John 4:24). This brief statement defines God as a spirit who is without tangible form.

After Jesus' resurrection, when He was showing His disciples that He had been raised bodily from the dead, He told them, "A spirit does not have flesh and bones as you see that I have" (Luke 24:39). As this applies to our understanding of who God is, we conclude that He does not possess a humanlike body with flesh and bones and skin. Possessing neither material bulk nor visible form, none of the properties of matter can be attributed to God. If you were to attempt to reach out to touch Him, there would be nothing to touch. If you were to look for Him, there would be nothing to see. He cannot be touched, felt, or seen because He is spirit.

BODY PARTS? NOT GOD!

If God is spirit and without a physical form, you may wonder about those passages in the Bible that portray God as having eyes (2 Chronicles 16:9; 1 Kings 8:29; Proverbs 15:3), hands (Ecclesiastes

9:1; Isaiah 65:2; Hebrews 1:10), ears (Nehemiah 1:6; Psalm 34:15), or feet (Genesis 3:8; Psalm 8:6). How are we to understand these verses? Although Scripture sometimes describes God in physical terms, we must understand that these anthropomorphic expressions are figures of speech.

In order to accommodate human weakness and our inability to grasp the sheer magnitude of His divine being, God has chosen to reveal Himself to us in human terms so that we can better grasp the incomprehensible truth about who He is. In no way are these anthropomorphic expressions intended to mean that God actually possesses physical body parts.

God does not possess a physical body with actual physical eyes, hands, ears, and feet. This imagery is used to reveal what God is *like,* not who God *is.* To say that God has hands means that He is powerful and strong. To say he has feet means that He moves about the earth and is everyplace. To say that He has eyes and ears means that He sees and hears everything. God is spirit without flesh and bones, and as such, is not bound by the finite of limitations of a human body.

So how important is it that God is spirit and not bound by physical limitations? Read on!

HE'S PRESENT EVERYWHERE

One specific implication of the reality that God is spirit is that He is able to be present everywhere at once. This doctrinal truth, called His omnipresence, means He is all-present in all His creation. If God possessed a physical body, He could occupy only one localized place at any one point in time. In other words, if God had a corporeal form, He could *not* be in two or more places at once. But because God is spirit, He is without the spatial limitations of a physical body. Recognizing His divine omnipresence, David asked:

Where can I go from Your Spirit?
Or where can I flee from Your presence?
If I ascend to heaven, You are there;
If I make my bed in hell, behold, You are there.
If I take the wings of the morning,
And dwell in the uttermost parts of the sea,
Even there Your hand shall lead me,
And Your right hand shall hold me.

PSALM 139:7-10, NKJV

David is saying there is no place where God is not always present. Whether it be north (heaven), south (Sheol), east (the dawn), or west (the sea), God is everywhere at the same time. In the words of one famous Puritan, "His center is everywhere, and His circumference is nowhere."

As a result of this wonderful truth, God is always near to us, an ever-present help in time of need. The psalmist declares:

God is our refuge and strength,
A very present help in trouble.

PSALM 46:1

More than being merely present, He is *very* present. God makes Himself available to those in need:

The LORD is near to all who call upon Him.

PSALM 145:18

Recognizing that He is always near, Moses asked, "For what great nation is there that has a god so near to it as is the LORD our God whenever we call on Him?" (Deuteronomy 4:7). No one is like our God, who is *always* present to help us when we call out to Him.

Has Anyone Seen God Lately?

Furthermore, because God is a spirit, He is invisible. We can see flesh and bones, but not a spirit being. When God appeared to His people in Old Testament times, they "did not see any form." Consequently, they were forbidden to make any visible image of Him (Deuteronomy 4:15–19).

The second commandment, as we discussed in the previous chapter, prohibits the making of any graven image or likeness of God. Because He is spirit, *any* visual representation of God would be a distortion of His true identity. Any picture, statue, or carving of Him who is invisible would only limit our thoughts about Him. God cannot be reduced to finite images. In fact, such attempts are sinful and a direct violation of Scripture.

In the New Testament, we read, "No one has seen God at any time" (John 1:18, NKJV). Paul calls Him "the invisible God" (Colossians 1:15) and says that "no man has seen or can see [Him]" (1 Timothy 6:16). The Bible is very clear: *God is invisible!*

But What About...?

You may be wondering: What about the Scriptures that say men saw God? What about Jacob, who said, "I have seen God face to face" (Genesis 32:30)? What about Moses who, along with Aaron, Nadab, Abihu, and the seventy elders of Israel, "saw the God of Israel" (Exodus 24:10)? What about Moses, to whom God said, "You shall see My back" (Exodus 33:23)? What about Isaiah, who said, "I saw the Lord" (Isaiah 6:1)?

Although I am digressing a bit, it is interesting to note that each of these instances when those men "saw" God is what theologians call a theophany or a Christophony, a preincarnate appearance of the second member of the Godhead, the Lord Jesus Christ. Long before Jesus came to this world two thousand years ago, He had already appeared to man by taking a bodily form. Such was clearly the case with both Jacob and Isaiah. These men did not see the first or third members of the Godhead, who are forever spirit. They saw the second member, Jesus Christ.

Jacob actually wrestled with the preincarnate Son of God, who momentarily took to Himself angelic features in order to appear to Jacob. Usually described as "the angel of the LORD," Jesus Christ visibly appeared to Abraham (Genesis 18:13–33; 22:11–18), Moses (Exodus 3:2–5), Gideon (Judges 6:11–23), and Elijah (1 Kings 19:5–7). Likewise, Isaiah saw the preincarnate Christ while he was in the temple (Isaiah 6:1). But God the Father? No one has ever seen Him because He is forever spirit. Nor has anyone ever seen God the Holy Spirit.

What about when Moses saw the Lord on Mount Sinai? To be accurate, God's servant merely saw the backside of God's glory, or the afterglow of His illuminated glory, which manifested itself as a bright light. But he did not actually see God. Instead, Moses saw God indirectly in the form of light, but not God Himself. (Exodus 33:22–23).

THE PERSONHOOD OF GOD

As we continue to frame an accurate picture of God, we must understand that God is a person, not an it. Never represented in the Bible as an impersonal force or an inanimate power, God is a person in the sense that He possesses all the characteristics of personality—mind, emotion, and will. In other words, God thinks, feels, and acts as He relates to His Creation.

Scripture refers to God by personal names such as Father, Friend, or Shepherd, and with personal pronouns such as I, Me, He, Him, and His. God's Word *never* uses the impersonal pronoun "it" to refer to Himself. God is a personal being who can be intimately known, loved, and adored. He relates to us as a person, and we can interact with Him as a living God. He listens to us, speaks to us, knows us, guides us, loves us, and can be grieved by us. Such can never be said of an impersonal force, inanimate object, or personified idea.

THE GOD WHO KNOWS

Continuing to develop our picture of God, we discover that He has an incomprehensible intellect with exponential powers of mental genius. God is perfect in insight, discernment, analysis, comparison, planning, inductive reasoning, deductive reasoning, and wisdom. With perfect powers of perception, He always knows all people, things, and events as they truly are. The Bible tells us, "There is no creature hidden from His sight, but all things are open and laid bare to the eyes of Him with whom we have to do" (Hebrews 4:13). God knows all things, even the secrets of men, our hidden works, our private thoughts, our unnoticed needs, and our unrevealed burdens.

Similarly, God even knows all things that would have occurred if another path had been followed. For example, Jesus knew that Tyre and Sidon would have repented had they seen the miracles that were done in Bethsaida and Chorazin, although that never actually occurred (Matthew 11:21). He also knew that Sodom and Gomorrah would have been spared had they seen the works that were done in Capernaum, which did not happen either (Matthew

11:23). So, God knows all things possible and actual—not only what is, but what might have been.

God Knew Tomorrow Yesterday

Enlarging our picture of God, we need to understand that He perfectly knows the future, whether it is of individuals, events, or nations. In fact, God knows the future so infinitely well that He has perfectly known all things about tomorrow from eternity past. Scripture declares that God is always:

> Declaring the end from the beginning
> And from ancient times things which have not been done.
>
> ISAIAH 46:10

Nothing about tomorrow is hidden from His sight today.

On this point, A. W. Pink once commented that God's knowledge of the future is as complete as is His knowledge of the past and the present because the future depends entirely upon Himself. He already knows the future because He has already designed and determined it. The only thing God foresees is what He has already foreordained (Acts 2:23; 4:27–28; 13:48).

Furthermore, God has never looked down the tunnel of time into the future to see what choice man would make. That is impossible because He has never learned anything. He knows all things immediately, simultaneously, exhaustively, and truly as they are. He gives attention to every minute detail: "His understanding is infinite" (Psalm 147:5). Even the hairs on our head are numbered (Matthew 10:30).

In addition, God is full of wisdom. He always knows what is best in every situation. With sheer genius beyond our ability to grasp, He created all that exists in His universe and continually governs all things with extraordinary intelligence. The prophet asks:

> Who has directed the Spirit of the LORD,
> Or as His counselor has informed Him?
> With whom did He consult
> and who gave Him understanding?
> And who taught Him in the path of justice
> and taught Him knowledge,
> And informed Him of the way of understanding?
>
> ISAIAH 40:13-14

The unmistakable answer is *no one*. God's knowledge is inexhaustible; His understanding is incomprehensible; His wisdom is inscrutable.

THE GOD WHO DEEPLY FEELS

Adding further brush strokes to our picture of God, we see that He possesses emotions and has extraordinary powers to feel with the greatest sensibility. We should never think of Him as if He were computerlike in His calculations, devoid of feelings, insensitive, callous, cold, stoic, or apathetic. Nothing could be further from the truth.

God always loves what is right and derives great pleasure from the good that conforms to His holy character. At the same time, He always hates what is evil and grieves at what fails to conform to Himself.

As a God who feels, He loves righteousness; and He also loves lost sinners who are made in His image. The psalmist declares, "You love righteousness and hate wickedness" (Psalm 45:7). With infinite passion, God is full of compassion for those in need of His grace (Psalm 111:4). Taking no pleasure in the death of the wicked (Ezekiel 33:11), He is slow to anger and touched with our infirmities (Psalm 103:8–9). As a father pities his children, so God greatly pities those who fear Him (Psalm 103:13).

On the other hand, He grieves over the sins of mankind. In the days of Noah, for example, sin caused God great sorrow (Genesis 6:6) because He is perfectly holy. He is a jealous God who is offended when not worshiped rightly (Exodus 20:5), and He becomes angry when He is dishonored (Deuteronomy 1:37). The Bible says He is the "God who has indignation every day" (Psalm 7:11). The psalmist says He hates "all who do iniquity.... The LORD abhors the man of bloodshed and deceit" (Psalm 5:5–6). Even believers grieve the Holy Spirit with sinful choices, hurtful attitudes, or evil actions (Ephesians 4:30). The point is that our sinful ways deeply wound God.

FROM ETERNITY TO ETERNITY

As we bring into focus an accurate picture of God, we see that the Bible also teaches that He is *eternal.* This means that He is infinite in relation to time and without beginning or end. As the eternal One, God is uncreated, the first cause of all things, yet He Himself was uncaused. There has never been a time when God did not exist. He is the original, preexistent cause of which everything else is the effect. He is before all things, the cause of time, reigning above time, for all time. Scripture identifies Him as "the Everlasting God" (Genesis 21:33). As such, there will never be a time when God will not exist. He will never cease being God—not now, not in the ages to come, not ever. The psalmist boasts, "From everlasting to everlasting, You are God" (Psalm 90:2, NKJV). The apostle Paul says that God "alone possesses immortality" (1 Timothy 6:16), meaning He lives forever.

GOD IS NOT CODEPENDENT

The Bible also teaches that God is *self-existent*. God is in no way dependent on anyone or anything outside of Himself. All things find their dependence on Him. When He chose to identify Himself as "I AM WHO I AM" (Exodus 3:14), God revealed to us, among other things, His self-existence. Contained in this divine name is the truth of His self-dependence, self-sufficiency, and self-reliance. As the great I AM, God reveals His independence and autonomy. By this, we mean that God has no needs that are unmet within Himself. Ultimately, He depends on no one or nothing else outside of Himself. God lacks nothing.

This is certainly contrary to the picture of today's user-friendly god. The popular and erroneous idea in our time is that we supply something that He lacks, as though God actually needs us. Some people imagine that God created humans to supply some need of His. They suppose that God was unfulfilled and needed to be loved or that He was lonely and needed company. Others imagine that we are absolutely necessary to carry out God's work of redemption— as if God somehow depends on us.

In one way or another, each of these views negates the essential truth that God is totally self-sufficient, autonomous, and independent. God was under no constraint, obligation, or necessity to create. The mere fact that God chose to create was because of Himself, and it was purely an act of His sovereign will. Why did God create? Simply because it pleased Him to do so.

GET THE PICTURE?

So, who really is God?

The answer comes, as we have seen, in the truth that God is spirit, invisible and infinite, everywhere present, eternal, self-existent, self-sufficient, a personal being with extraordinary powers of genius, feeling, and choosing. He alone is the primary cause of which everything else is the subsequent effect. Uncreated, He is not dependent on anyone or anything else. Rather, we all find our dependency on Him who alone is perfect and glorious.

This is who God is!

To view God in any other fashion is to misunderstand Him. Our thoughts about God must conform to the reality of who He is. Only as we search the Scripture and apply ourselves to the pursuit of knowing His true nature will our lives enjoy the fullness of His presence.

chapter five

WHOLLY, WHOLLY HOLY!

The Holiness of God

—

Holiness is the most sparkling
jewel of His crown; it is the name
by which God is known.

THOMAS WATSON

As the former pastor of the historic Tenth Presbyterian Church in downtown Philadelphia, Donald Grey Barnhouse was one of the great Bible teachers of the twentieth century. An alumnus of Princeton Theological Seminary, early in his ministry he was invited back to campus to preach in Miller Chapel.

As Barnhouse stood to preach, Dr. Robert Dick Wilson, one of the renowned professors at Princeton and a brilliant scholar, took his seat in the front row, which the young preacher found somewhat intimidating. Understandably, Barnhouse felt fear and trepidation about teaching the Scriptures to those who had taught him.

At the close of the message, Dr. Wilson approached Barnhouse and announced, "If you come back again, I will *not* come to hear you preach." Barnhouse collapsed on the inside. How had he failed? Was his theology wrong? Was his use of the original languages improper?

With all the courage he could muster, the young preacher asked the aged professor, "Where did I fail?"

"Fail?" Wilson replied. "Oh, you didn't fail. I only come to hear a former student once. I only want to know if he is a big-Godder or a little-Godder, and then I know how his ministry will be."

When his former student asked for an explanation, Wilson answered, "Some men have a little God, and they are always in trouble with Him. He can't do any miracles. He can't take care of the inspiration and transmission of the Scripture. He doesn't intervene on behalf of His people. They have a little God, and I call them little-Godders.

"There are others who have a great God," Wilson continued. "He speaks, and it is done. He commands, and it stands fast. He knows how to show Himself strong on behalf of them that fear Him. You are a big-Godder, and He will bless your ministry." He paused a moment, smiled, and walked out.

What a lesson for Barnhouse!

What a lesson for *us!*

BEING A BIG-GODDER

Big-Godders believe in a great God and do great things for Him. According to His eternal purpose, God delights in taking ordinary people who believe that He is big and doing extraordinary things through them. This way the glory belongs to Him, not to man. The key for making one's life count for time and eternity is to be gripped with a high view of God and then to be sold out for Him. The Bible says, "The people who know their God will display strength and take action" (Daniel 11:32).

So, what is the essential key to becoming a big-Godder? What is the primary truth about God that we must grasp if we are to have a high view of Him? More than any other of His divine attributes, God has revealed Himself to us as being absolutely holy. Arguably, God's holiness is the most important of all His attributes. It constitutes the core of His nature, the essence of His being, and the crown of His character. If our thoughts of God are to be worthy, the primary truth that should govern how we perceive Him is that He alone is perfectly holy. If we are to properly understand who He is, we must grasp the true meaning of this central aspect of His divine being.

USER-FRIENDLY SHALLOWNESS

My heartfelt concern for the church today is that God's holiness is a forgotten attribute. I believe this because I am convinced that there is too much shallowness and irreverence these days regarding God. If the user-friendly god falls short anywhere, it is in regard to divine holiness. To hear many people talk today, God is a *happy* God, a *helpful* God, a *laughing* God. But a *holy* God? Hardly! Turn on the average Christian broadcast; read the average Christian book; listen to the average Christian speaker—you will probably not be awestruck with a sense of God's holiness.

Instead of being absolutely holy, our user-friendly god is casual, common, and congenial. Regarding God as loveable and good-natured may evoke warm, fuzzy feelings, but it will not lead to triumphant faith. This picture of God brings Him down to our level and makes Him so buddy-buddy that we fail to understand the majestic transcendence of His awesome holiness.

THE TRIVIALIZATION OF GOD

Unfortunately, this shallow view of God has led to the shocking trend of trivializing His awesome holiness in church worship. Much worship in our congregations these days shows little regard for God's holiness and thus falls dreadfully short of giving Him the praise due His name. Sentimental emotions abound, but there is little true reverence. The astonished wonder and respectful awe reserved for a God who is holy and beyond our comprehension has been replaced with syrupy, feel-good, devotional thoughts about God. Such is the legacy of the user-friendly god—irreverence, superficiality, and even carnality.

There is certainly a place for a warm, loving approach to God—for those feelings of devotion. When you read the Psalms, you hear David singing and rejoicing before God. Obviously, there were some deep emotions flowing from this "man after God's own heart." But David never lost sight of God's awesome holiness. Nor should we! We need to be mindful of the fact that our worship of God will be only as high and deep and great as are our thoughts of Him. At the center of our worthy thoughts of God must be towering, transforming thoughts of His holiness.

With this in mind, our focus will now turn to understanding God's holiness, the chief attribute that encompasses the whole of His being. We need to ask: In what ways is God holy? And how should we think of Him as holy? Does God operate from an inflexible, holy standard? We must give careful answers to these critical questions if we are to come to understand His holiness.

HE'S A CUT ABOVE!

Any discussion of God's holiness must begin with clarifying the meaning of the word *holy*. This is a word that is often used but seldom understood. Its essential meaning is "separate" or "separateness." The word is derived from a Semitic root that means "to cut, to separate," like cutting an object in half to separate the two halves. Literally, holiness means that something or someone is cut away from, set apart, and separated.

As it relates to the Bible, the word *holy* is used in two different ways, with a primary and secondary meaning. First and foremost, holiness means that God is a cut above us, infinitely transcendent, above and beyond His creation. He is totally distinct from us, one of a kind, and, therefore, cannot be compared with anyone or anything else because He vastly exceeds all comparisons. Even though the Bible tells us we are "made in His image," that divine likeness within us has definite limitations because God is totally set apart from us, different from us, above us.

The prophet wrote, "To whom then will you liken God? Or what likeness will you compare with Him?" (Isaiah 40:18). The obvious answer is no one! He is so exalted in His holiness, so elevated above His creation that there is no basis for comparison between Him and us. The chasm is infinite.

PERFECT IN JUDGMENT, PERFECT IN ACTIONS

The secondary meaning of the word *holy,* as it applies to God, is that He is free from any stain of sin and is wholly perfect. God has never done anything wrong and never will. He is without error in all His ways. He *never* makes a misjudgment. He *never* causes something to happen that is not right. Like a flawless diamond, God is utterly, absolutely perfect (Matthew 5:48).

Taking this a step further, the holiness of God demands that He judge sin (Exodus 34:7). Not only does He perfectly love righteousness, God also has a perfect, pure hatred of sin. He cannot tolerate any unrighteousness or overlook iniquity. With unblemished purity, God's holiness demands that He pour out His wrath on everything that does not conform to His own perfect character. It is only because of God's own grace that He can associate Himself with sinful humankind.

This is the holiness of God, the foundational truth of all truths about Him.

In order to get a better grasp of this divine attribute, let us now conduct a brief survey of Scripture regarding God's holiness. What we will discover from cover to cover is that holiness is an essential part of God's revelation of Himself to us.

GOD'S HOLY HABITATION

God's habitation in heaven is a holy place. This means the place where God dwells is free from the contamination of sin. God's throne room of glory is perfectly pure, unstained by any evil. This reflects the very character of God Himself. Thus, to be in God's holy presence, one must be absolutely holy.

Lucifer, the highest of the angels with the closest proximity to God's holiness, sinned by seeking to elevate himself above God's throne. Because of this prideful rebellion, God said, "You will be thrust down to Sheol, to the recesses of the pit" (Isaiah 14:15). In addition, God said:

> "Your heart was lifted up because of your beauty;
> You corrupted your wisdom by reason of your splendor.
> I cast you to the ground."
> EZEKIEL 28:17

Because of God's own holiness, this sin *had* to be judged, and God banished Lucifer from His glorious presence forever. Thus, He preserved the holiness of His throne room in heaven. The lesson is clear: God is absolutely holy, pure, and undefiled, and those who would dwell in His presence must be holy as He is holy.

GOD'S HOLY CREATION

In a similar way, God demonstrated His holiness when He created the world without any trace of sin. Regarding all that He made, God declared that it was very good (Genesis 1:31). Our world was once completely free of sin and corruption. But, as a result of the seductive temptation of Satan, Adam and Eve sinned, causing God to drive them away from His holy presence in the Garden. Scripture says, "He drove the man out; and at the east of the garden of Eden He stationed the cherubim, and the flaming sword which turned every direction, to guard the way to the tree of life" (Genesis 3:24).

Adam and Eve's sin forfeited for them—and for us—the privilege of being in God's holy presence. Their rebellion placed between a holy God and His sinful mankind a gulf—an *infinite* gulf—because His holiness cannot fellowship with our unholiness. The Bible tells us, "For what partnership have righteousness and lawlessness, or what fellowship has light with darkness?" (2 Corinthians 6:14). The answer is *none!*

Because of sin, unrepentant sinners are separated from God forever and will be sent "into the eternal fire which has been prepared for the devil and his angels" (Matthew 25:41). Throughout all eternity future, God will fellowship only with those who are made perfectly holy in His sight. To fail to grasp this reality is to fail to grasp how holy He is and how unholy we are.

God's Holy Ground

The first time the word *holy* is used in the Bible is in Exodus 3 where we read of Moses' encounter with God at the burning bush. While tending his father-in-law's flock, Moses came to a mountain called Horeb and saw a bush that was on fire. As Moses drew near to it, he discovered something very strange: The plant was burning, but the fire was not consuming it. Then, from the midst of this burning bush, God called to him, saying, "Moses, Moses!" Understandably startled, Moses replied, "Here I am." God then made a most significant statement: "Do not come near here; remove your sandals from your feet, for the place on which you are standing is holy ground" (v. 5).

Think about this for a moment. God declared that *the ground* on which Moses stood was *holy*. What did that mean? The dirt itself had no intrinsic virtue; it was just dirt. But this place was now special because God Himself was there. The fact that He declared this ground holy meant the place where Moses now stood was set apart and sacred because God's presence was uniquely manifested there. Wherever the divine presence is revealed, that place is immediately sanctified.

The removal of one's sandals was a sign of reverence in a holy place, acknowledging one's unworthiness to be present. It was a recognition of the infinite holiness of the God who was there.

Invited by God Himself into His awesome presence, Moses did not come flippantly. Instead, he approached the Holy One with lowly submission, humble contrition, and reverential awe. When God identified Himself as "the God of your father, the God of Abraham, the God of Isaac, and the God of Jacob" (v. 6), Moses covered his face in fear, afraid even to look at God. Although God had extended this access into His holy presence, Moses was traumatized by his proximity to deity, and rightly so.

I wonder, have we lost a sense of God's awesome holiness in the church today? Instead of approaching God as Moses did—with an appropriate sense of awe—we seem to do all we can to make ourselves feel as comfortable as possible in His divine presence, rather than feeling contrite or convicted. In the average church the only sweating palms are those of the soloist who stands to sing. The only shaking knees are those of the pastor as he prepares to deliver his sermon. But an intimidating sense of divine holiness? Hardly. Sad to say, we all too often are far from it. Where is our reverence and awe? Not until we regain a healthy sense of God's absolute holiness will we regain a healthy sense of godly fear.

Reverencing God does not negate rejoicing in Him. In fact, it contributes to our celebration in the greatness of who He is. But we must never forget that the fear of the Lord truly is the beginning of wisdom (Proverbs 1:7; 9:10). Only when we first fear Him can we properly rejoice in Him.

GOD'S HOLY MOUNTAIN

As we delve deeper into God's holiness, we discover that this divine attribute was further revealed at Mount Sinai after Moses had led the nation of Israel out of Egyptian bondage (Exodus 19). As God's people camped at the base of the mountain, Moses climbed to the summit to meet with God. There the Lord instructed him to tell the people to consecrate themselves to Him, wash their clothes, and be ready for the third day when He would powerfully come down upon Mount Sinai and make Himself known.

This mountain where God was to appear would be so holy that anyone who even touched it was to be put to death (v. 12). Not even an animal could enter God's sacred presence and live. By imposing the death penalty, God was teaching them that He was not to be approached flippantly or casually.

On the third day, thunder erupted; lightning struck; a thick cloud descended; and the deafening blast of a trumpet sounded. This dramatic manifestation of God's holiness caused the people to tremble with fear. Encountering this same God today—a *holy* God—should still elicit reverential awe and godly fear from the hearts of His people.

Like a red-hot furnace spewing out smoke, Mount Sinai was engulfed in billowing, dark clouds as fire burned on the mountainside and God made known to His people His awesome holiness. The mountain shook; the ground quaked; and the trumpet blast grew louder. In unmistakable fashion, God was revealing that He is not to be approached casually, but only with deep reverence and a healthy fear.

The psalmist proclaims:

> Worship the LORD in holy attire;
> Tremble before Him, all the earth.
>
> PSALM 96:9

His holiness should inspire our worship, wonder, and awe. Whatever happened to reverential awe?

GOD'S HOLY LAW

When God gave His law to Moses at Mount Sinai, He further manifested His holiness. In the Ten Commandments, He revealed His utter separateness and moral purity in the requirements He placed on His people (Exodus 20:1–17). He declared they were not to have any other gods before Him, construct any man-made image of Him, use His name in vain, or forget the Sabbath as a day of worship. Instead, they were to keep His name holy—set apart.

In addition, God gave them the design of the tabernacle, which was to become their central place of worship (Exodus 25–31; 35–40). God designed this portable tent, which contained the Holy Place and the Most Holy Place, to teach that He is separate from all His Creation. This underscored the truth that, as the Holy One—transcendent, majestic, totally set apart from all mankind, removed from everything unclean or evil—God dwells in infinite purity.

God also issued the sacrificial law, which further revealed His holiness (Leviticus 1–7). He instructed His people that He could only be approached with a sacrifice for sin, further testifying that He is so holy He cannot be accessed without a covering for sin. God dwells in unapproachable light, which no man has seen or can see (1 Timothy 6:16). Only through the sacrifice of Christ for our sins can we come boldly before His throne. Even at that, we must never draw near without reverence and awe.

GOD'S HOLY THRONE

As we continue to examine God's holiness, we come to what may be the single most dramatic encounter with it that any individual has ever had. We will study this scene later in greater detail, but I want to consider it briefly now.

After the death of King Uzziah, the prophet Isaiah went to the temple to seek the Lord. In that hour of crisis, God gave Isaiah an extraordinary vision—one that radically changed his life and ministry. Indeed, it would be impossible to imagine radical changes *not* taking place in the life of someone who saw what Isaiah saw.

In this encounter, the prophet "saw the Lord sitting on a throne, lofty and exalted, with the train of His robe filling the temple" (Isaiah 6:1). Isaiah saw heaven's King exalted, enthroned, majestic, high and lifted up. Above His throne, the prophet saw a host of angelic beings called seraphim engaged in fervent praise. With two wings, they covered their feet; with two wings, they covered their face; with two wings, they flew. No wonder these heavenly creatures covered their feet and faces! In the presence of the thrice-holy God, these seraphim were directly exposed to His full glory, a sight too blinding for any creature to withstand.

Then, Isaiah heard these angelic beings cry out:

> "Holy, Holy, Holy, is the LORD of hosts,
> The whole earth is full of His glory."
> ISAIAH 6:3

With intentional repetition, the angels echoed this description of divine greatness three times, communicating the superlative degree. This one divine perfection—*holiness*—is the only attribute recorded in Scripture with a three-fold emphasis, meaning God is holy, holier, holiest—the *holiest* being in all the universe. Day and night, these seraphim praise Him for who He truly is—*holy*. What a picture this paints of God's holiness!

Note that the angels did not cry out, "Loving, Loving, Loving," nor did they exclaim "Immutable, Immutable, Immutable," although God is certainly those things to an infinite degree. These angelic beings exclaimed, "Holy, Holy, Holy," affirming that holiness is the one divine attribute singled out and raised to the highest degree. More than any other attribute, holiness is the centerpiece of His divine being and captures the true essence of God. Out of God's holiness flows everything that He is.

From this, we may conclude that, more than anything else, God is holy. He is transcendent, majestic, high and lifted up, exalted above all, enthroned over all, sinless, absolutely pure, perfect in all His ways.

This is God's holiness.

GOD'S HOLY SON

As awesome as this demonstration of God's holiness is, there is one that surpasses it. It is when God Himself became a man and walked among us. The greatest demonstration of God's holiness is unquestionably found in the coming of His Son, Jesus Christ, the holy offspring (Luke 1:35).

Although tempted in all things as we are, Jesus nevertheless lived a sinless, perfect life. The Bible says that He was without sin (Hebrews 4:15), "knew no sin" (2 Corinthians 5:21), and that He appeared as the One who was "holy, innocent, undefiled, separated from sinners" (Hebrews 7:26). Peter declared Him as "the Holy and Righteous One" (Acts 3:14), and demons recognized Him as "the Holy One of God" (Luke 4:34) in whom "there is no sin" (1 John 3:5). He "committed no sin, nor was any deceit found in His mouth" (1 Peter 2:22).

Jesus spent His life on earth demonstrating His holiness in the words He spoke, in how He lived, in the miracles He performed. As the Son of God, He understood that His only purpose for coming to earth was to demonstrate God's holiness to those with whom He came in contact. Not everyone recognized that holiness, but those who were closest to Christ quickly realized whose presense they were in.

Peter understood that he was in the presence of holy God after the first miraculous catch of fish. Falling to his knees, he said, "Depart from me, for I am a sinful man, O Lord!" (Luke 5:8). When confronted with divine holiness in Christ, all he could see was his own wretched sinfulness.

Jesus spoke with wisdom, proclaiming the Word of God before all mankind. He performed miracles, offered God's forgiveness to those who believed, and gave Himself as an example of what a godly life looks like. All of these things were demonstrations of the holiness of God.

But there was one more thing He did that stands as the ultimate demonstration of God's holiness.

HOLINESS AT THE CROSS

The greatest revelation of God's holiness in Christ occurred at the cross when Jesus died to satisfy God's requirements for holiness. By bearing our sins as the sinless Lamb of God, Jesus—God's own Son, who became sin for us—endured the full measure of God's wrath and holy judgment. Being perfectly holy, God turned His back on His own Son as He bore our sins. That is why Jesus cried out, "My God, My God, why have You forsaken Me?" (Matthew 27:46, NKJV).

Think about that for a moment. God forsook His own Son, the second member of the Godhead with whom He had enjoyed perfect fellowship from eternity past. God the Father, because He could not look on the sin that Jesus had in effect become, turned away from His own Son. The Lord Jesus Christ was obedient to His heavenly Father to the point of willingly dying the most horrible, grisly death imaginable. Because of His obedience to the Father, He was abandoned at the cross, left to die so that we might live.

That's how *holy* God is.

When His own beloved Son became sin for us, God could not fellowship with Him. If God rejected Christ upon the cross, He will surely reject every other person who dies in his or her sins. Only through faith in the death and resurrection of Christ can we be made holy and enjoy fellowship with God. When we believe in Christ, God imputes His own perfect holiness to us, enabling Him to receive us into His holy presence as He does His own Son. When we believe in Christ, God gives us a perfect standing before Him. Herein, the holiness of God is revealed. When we believe in Christ, God's perfect purity is imparted to us (2 Corinthians 5:21).

FIRST IMPRESSION, LASTING IMPRESSION

I remind you, what comes to your mind when you begin to think about God is the most important thing about you. The first thought to enter your mind should be His holiness. Holy, holy, holy is the Lord! Set apart from all His creation, He alone is truly transcendent, majestic, lofty, exalted, high and lifted up, pure, without sin, without error—in a word, *perfect*—perfect in His character, words, and deeds.

Of all His divine attributes, holiness is the one that most uniquely describes Him. In reality, it summarizes all His other attributes. So, no matter how other people may characterize Him, let us affirm His utter, absolute, perfect, infinite holiness. To perceive Him in any other way is to take the first step toward idolatry and worshiping a god of our own making. And a man-centered god, created in our own image and less than absolutely holy, is no god at all.

God *is* wholly, wholly *holy!*

chapter six

HE IS THE KING!

The Sovereignty of God

---

*Divine sovereignty simply
means that God is God.*

A. W. PINK

N apoleon Bonaparte was once asked, "Is God on the side
of France?" Intoxicated with the power of his own success, this famed military leader arrogantly replied, "God
is on the side that has the heaviest artillery." By that he meant that
it did not matter what God willed, but what *he* willed. Later, this
diminutive dictator boasted, "*I* make circumstances."

But that was before Waterloo.

In 1815, Napoleon's army advanced across Europe into
Belgium to trounce the armies of Britain and Russia. But despite his
superior weaponry, the "Little Corporal" lost both the battle and his
empire. In an unexpected, ignominious defeat, this humbled
emperor was unseated from his throne and exiled to the barren
island of St. Helena a chastened man.

As he contemplated his military losses, Napoleon changed his
perspective about God, his life, and history. No longer boasting that

God is on the side that possesses the greatest human strength, he began singing a different tune. Quoting the words of Thomas à Kempis, this once-proud man acknowledged, "Man proposes, but God disposes."

GOD ALONE CONTROLS ALL THINGS

Napoleon learned a valuable lesson, one that each one of us must grasp. God—not man or circumstances—is sovereign; and He rules over the affairs of all people, from the greatest to the least. Following His own divinely written script, God controls history, no matter how man may try to assert himself. God, enthroned in the heavens, governs all, even the rulers of this world, and is accomplishing His royal will in our lives.

One of the fundamental truths in the Bible is this teaching that God is sovereign. By this, we mean God reigns over all His creation, governing and guiding all things to their divinely appointed end. Although, from a human perspective, it may appear otherwise, He is in charge of the universe, exercising absolute control over all things. As our sovereign Lord, He does *always* as He pleases, *only* as He pleases, and *all* that He pleases.

Thus, to say that God is sovereign is simply to say that He is God.

A DETHRONED DEITY

Sadly, there is another picture of God—one that presents a user-friendly image of God.

We seldom hear about the sovereign God today. Even when people speak of God's autonomous authority, they often do not fully understand what it is. The user-friendly god is like Napoleon—a monarch in exile. A dethroned deity, he appears to have exchanged his throne of sovereignty for a footstool of subordination to the will of his creation.

In the minds of so many people today, even some in the body of Christ, the user-friendly god has voluntarily limited his control and given free reign to the actions of people in order to give them unconditional liberty. This restricted ruler is *slightly* sovereign— enthroned, but not empowered; presiding, but not prevailing; trying, but not triumphing.

In the views of many, God is always pacing back and forth in heaven, wringing His hands over unfolding events on earth, rubbing His furrowed brow, and losing sleep over His plans, which are being repeatedly frustrated by men. They see him as continually going into an emergency session with the other members of the Trinity, strategizing His next move, always reacting to the next hand dealt to Him by man, Satan, or circumstances.

Some believe that divine sovereignty is a sort of coregency—a cosmic stalemate between God and Satan in which man has the swing vote. These well-meaning people spout catchy idioms like, "God votes for you; the devil votes against you; and you cast the deciding vote." This implies that God and Satan are somehow equals and that man's will is superior to both, since he is able to cast the tie-breaking vote for heaven or hell.

God is too often perceived as a codependent deity who is always rigging solutions to earthly problems, but who, quite frankly, lacks the clout to pull it off. This is the user-friendly god. But is *this* God? Has He really chosen to limit the free reign of His sovereignty? Is He limited by the choices of man? Or is God really the supreme ruler of the universe, exercising total control over all the works of His hand?

Rest assured, God is in complete control!

IT'S THIS SIMPLE: GOD IS GOD!

From cover to cover, the Bible uncompromisingly and consistently teaches the absolute sovereignty of God. The Word tells us that God is infinitely elevated above His creation, the Lord of heaven and earth, subject to none, influenced by none, accountable to none. The psalmist declares, "Our God is in the heavens; He does whatever He pleases" (Psalm 115:3). Speaking through the prophet Isaiah, God said, "My counsel shall stand, and I will do all My pleasure" (Isaiah 46:10, NKJV). By this statement, God claims to be the sovereign Lord of heaven and earth, always carrying forward His will.

Now, that is the *true* God of the Bible!

Every realm of God's creation is subject to His decrees, every atom obedient to His authority, every devil governed by His edicts, every human controlled by His desires. God reigns freely over all that He has made. As we will discover, God is on His throne and "works all things after the counsel of His will" (Ephesians 1:11). Let us survey each of these areas.

HE'S IN CONTROL OF THE CREATION

The fact that God simply spoke the world into being clearly demonstrates His sovereignty over all He created. Being under no coercion by anyone or anything, God the Father, Son, and Holy Spirit existed by Himself from eternity past. Free to create or to not create, in an extraordinary display of sheer sovereignty, God spoke this universe and all it contains into existence.

Every single dimension of creation is but a silent testimony to the supreme authority of God. The mere fact that He created *what* He wanted, *when* He wanted it, and *as* He wanted it is a strong statement of God's absolute right to do as He pleases. From whom did He receive permission to create? No one! He chose to create, by Himself and for Himself.

To this day, God has not relinquished His sovereign prerogative to govern what He has made. Having spoken into being everything that exists, God continually sustains and rules over His universe. Contrary to what many believe, He has not made this world and then adopted a hands-off policy, choosing to withdraw His control and allow whatever happens to happen on its own. The universe is not a top that God spun into existence and is now watching unwind from a distance. Instead, God directly governs all His crea-tion, orchestrating all nations, people, events, and circumstances, causing all things to work together for His glory and our good.

ALL NATURE BOWS BEFORE HIM

The outworking of natural occurrences, whether peaceful or violent, belongs to the hand of God. Scripture reveals that God exhibits His power over all the forces of nature. The Lord has established the physical laws by which He governs the forces of nature, and these laws continually operate according to His sustaining power. For example, all types of weather—from a gentle rain to a devastating flood—are the result of the controlling, sovereign hand of God. He does not merely intervene on specific occasions; He rules over all of nature every day.

Affirming God's active control over nature, Jesus said that God "causes His sun to rise on the evil and the good, and sends rain on the righteous and the unrighteous" (Matthew 5:45). Who sends the sunshine and rain, as well as every other form of weather? According to Jesus, God does. He unleashes the lightning and directs the snow, rain, and clouds (Job 37:3–13). Even deadly storms, violent tornadoes, and severe hurricanes are under God's direction. Earthquakes, famines, and floods, referred to by insurance companies as "acts of God," are just that—acts of God!

Only God can control what man cannot—the weather. In order to illustrate this, Luke 8:22–25 tells us the story of Jesus calming a terrible storm. Jesus was in a boat with His disciples on the Sea of Galilee, sleeping in the bow, when a violent storm arose. The disciples' fear increased with each cresting wave. Finally, in a state of panic because their lives were in danger, they woke their sleeping Master. With audacious authority, Christ, as God incarnate, stood and "rebuked the wind and the surging waves" (v. 24). At that exact moment, the wind ceased and the sea stilled.

Such is His power over nature, day by day, in all places.

THE POWER BEHIND EARTHLY THRONES

God's control of earthly events is not limited to natural occurrences. His sovereignty extends to worldly power structures as well.

By divine authority, God makes all of the decisions of rulers and governments work together to conform to His plan for human history. He is King of kings and Lord of lords, ruling over all earthly rulers, governing all governors, dictating to all dictators, leading all leaders.

God determines *who* assumes office, as well as *when* and *where* they preside over peoples. The Bible notes, "He removes kings and establishes kings" (Daniel 2:21). No ruler, good or evil, rules apart from God's will. The Bible says:

> The Most High is ruler over the realm of mankind,
> And bestows it on whom He wishes,
> And sets over it the lowliest of men.
>
> DANIEL 4:17

This means that God confers earthly authority on whomever He pleases, even if He chooses to give it to the weakest of men. In such cases, there can be no reasonable explanation except that God did it. The psalmist agrees:

> For not from the east, nor from the west,
> Nor from the desert comes exaltation;
> But God is the Judge;
> He puts down one, and exalts another.
>
> PSALM 75:6–7

This is *God*—removing one human ruler, raising up another.

Once they are in office, God determines *how* they lead. With undeniable clarity, Solomon writes:

> The king's heart is like channels of water
> in the hand of the LORD;
> He turns it wherever He wishes.
>
> PROVERBS 21:1

We should not minimize the force of this verse, but we must allow the Bible to mean what it says. This passage clearly states that all earthly kings, leaders, and rulers are subject to God's direct intervention and are subordinate to His divine control. Even evil tyrants, self-willed dictators, and corrupt politicians carry out their duties within the inscrutable, sovereign will of God. God is His own purpose. He alone knows His sovereign ways, and He works through leaders—yes, even *wicked* leaders—to carry out His eternal purposes.

THE INVISIBLE, SOVEREIGN HAND

God works on a grander scale than what meets the human eye. Recognizing His invisible hand at work behind the scenes, Ezra wrote that the Lord "turned the heart of the king of Assyria toward them [the Jews] to encourage them in the work of the house of God" (Ezra 6:22). From this we can conclude that God Himself, the one true Ruler, governed this unbelieving king's every decision, whether directly causing it or divinely permitting it. It was God who "put such a thing as this in the king's heart, to adorn the house of the LORD" (Ezra 7:27). In this instance, God used a pagan potentate to assist in the restoration of His own house of worship.

So complete is God's control over unbelieving monarchs that He referred to Cyrus, the pagan ruler of Persia, as "My shepherd" who "will perform all My desire." Although Cyrus was an unconverted ruler, God referred to him as the one "whom I have taken by the right hand" (Isaiah 44:28–45:1). From this, we learn that God rules *all* earthly rulers—even unregenerate kings—to carry out His purposes on a global scale. He even raised up Pharaoh, the Egyptian ruler, and used him to bring glory to His own name.

THE OUTCOME IS FROM GOD

Once God puts earthly rulers into office, He determines their successes and defeats. Acknowledging God's right to give or withhold military victory in the day of battle, Solomon observed, "The horse is prepared for the day of battle, but victory belongs to the LORD"

(Proverbs 21:31). The psalmist meant the same thing when he wrote:

> The king is not saved by a mighty army;
> A warrior is not delivered by great strength.
> A horse is a false hope for victory;
> Nor does it deliver anyone by its great strength.
>
> PSALM 33:16–17

No matter how powerful a king may be, success ultimately comes from the Lord, not man. The psalmist also said:

> Some boast in chariots, and some in horses;
> But we will boast in the name of the LORD, our God.
>
> PSALM 20:7

The battle, specifically its outcome, belongs to the Lord!

God rules over all mankind, from the greatest to the smallest. He governs not only the high and mighty, but also every person of lesser power and influence. If He can control those upon earthly thrones, how much more must He rule over those of us who are subject to earthly powers!

God governs on a microlevel as well as a macrolevel. "Are not two sparrows sold for a cent?" Jesus asked. "And yet not one of them will fall to the ground apart from your Father" (Matthew 10:29). According to our Lord, not even a small bird dies apart from our Father's will. In every single event, no matter how minute, God exercises His sovereign control—even over the existence of a sparrow. God oversees the life of every single person, who, Jesus tells us, is of far greater value to God than a sparrow.

Properly understood, this truth leads not to deadly fatalism, but to dynamic faith!

HE'S SOVEREIGN OVER THE ENEMY

Perhaps the greatest misconception of God's sovereignty concerns His dealings with Satan. Some view God and Satan as two heavyweight boxers in the ring, fighting it out, with God barely prevailing in the last round by a split decision.

Nothing could be farther from the truth. By the very definition of the word, there can be only one sovereign. Victorious in every realm of His dealings with Satan, God has decisively trounced the devil, making him an already defeated foe, under the sure sentence of judgment. In short, the battle is all but over, and the outcome has been decided!

As we apply biblical focus to our lives, we can see that Satan is eternally and entirely subordinate to God's prerogatives. In the very beginning, God created Satan as Lucifer, the highest of all the angels in glory, endowed with extraordinary gifts, dazzling beauty, and vast wisdom (Ezekiel 28:11–15). He was given the closest proximity to God's throne, but therein lay the problem. Instead of remaining subservient to God, he rose up in rebellion, seeking to overthrow Him. Filled with pride, Lucifer sought to exalt himself above God's throne (Isaiah 14:12–14) and led one-third of the angels in a cosmic revolt against Him (Revelation 12:4). As anarchical as this action was, God planned and permitted it according to His perfect, sovereign will, yet without being the author of sin.

There can be only *one* sovereign. Acting in holy judgment, God banished Lucifer from heaven, exiling him to earth, where he is now "the ruler of this world" (John 12:31) and "the god of this age" (2 Corinthians 4:4, NKJV). In a state of perpetual rebellion against God, Satan is nevertheless subject to God's control, unable to overcome God's sovereign will. Granted, Satan can and does create hellish havoc and cause great trouble, but *only* to the extent God allows him and that often at God's own initiative (Job 1–2). In other words, Satan is like a dog on God's chain—going no farther and doing no more evil than God permits.

As a defeated foe, Satan has been cast down from heaven (Luke 10:18), cursed in the Garden (Genesis 3:15), defeated at the cross (Colossians 2:15), and is awaiting his execution at the final judgment (Revelation 20:10). Until then, God exercises absolute authority over the devil, monitoring and regulating his every move, using him as a mere pawn to accomplish His own eternal purposes.

NOTHING "JUST HAPPENS"

In governing the universe, God controls all occurrences, events, and actions. It may seem to some people that this world is out of control—but such is not the case. Tragedies come; trials buffet us; the unexpected occurs. Yet, despite outward appearances, God fully controls all events and brings all occurrences to their appointed end. This is often called the doctrine of providence, or the truth that God orders all events according to His eternal plan.

The apostle Paul declared this grand truth when He wrote, "And we know that God causes all things to work together for good to those who love God, to those who are called according to His purpose" (Romans 8:28). By this, Paul affirms that according to God's sovereign decree, He orchestrates every circumstance in life—even suffering, temptation, and sin—to accomplish His glory and our good, which is to conform us to Christ's image. So it is clear, God "works all things after the counsel of His will" (Ephesians 1:11).

There is no such thing as random chance, good luck, or blind fate—because absolutely nothing happens apart from God's control. From the divine perspective, there are no accidents. The Bible says:

> The lot is cast into the lap,
> But its every decision is from the LORD.
> PROVERBS 16:33

This means that even the tossing of the lot, much like throwing dice, is under the directing control of God's invisible hand.

OUR DAYS ARE NUMBERED

God has numbered our days, and He directs our lives. Every aspect of our existence, from the time of our birth to the length of our days, is divinely orchestrated according to God's master plan. Psalm 139:16 says, "And in Your book were all written the days that were ordained for me, when as yet there was not one of them." God recorded all the days that we have to live in His book of providence long before we entered this world.

Obviously then, God is sovereign over the beginning of our days. By determining the time of every human birth, God dictates when we step onto the stage of human history. It was said regarding Hannah that "the LORD had closed her womb" (1 Samuel 1:5), while He opened the womb of Leah (Genesis 29:31). Sarah, Abraham's wife, said, "The LORD has prevented me from bearing children" (Genesis 16:2); while the angel of the LORD said to Zacharius, "Your petition has been heard, and your wife Elizabeth will bear you a son" (Luke 1:13). These Scriptures teach that God controls the conception of children.

Furthermore, God determines to *whom* and *where* on the globe a child will be born. Obviously, an unborn child does not have a say in these matters. But neither is it left to chance. Rather, all of these details are a part of a larger master plan that God designed with inscrutable wisdom.

God even superintends the physical and emotional formation of every child conceived. The Psalmist said:

> For You have formed my inward parts;
> You have covered me in my mother's womb.
> I will give praise You, for I am fearfully and wonderfully made;
> Marvelous are Your works, and that my soul knows very well.
> My frame was not hidden from You, when I was made in secret,
> And skillfully wrought in the lowest parts of the earth.
> Your eyes saw my substance.
>
> PSALM 139:13–16, NKJV

God's sovereignty is clearly displayed in the formation of a human body in the mother's womb before birth. God sovereignly fashions each child exactly as He has designed while he or she is still in the womb.

AN APPOINTED TIME

On the other end of the spectrum of life, God controls the timing and circumstances of our deaths. We have a divinely appointed number of days in which to live, and we cannot exceed that amount by one day.

The most vivid illustration of this truth is the crucifixion of Jesus Christ. According to Scripture, there was an appointed hour for Christ to go to the cross and die for our sins. He died at exactly the predetermined time, not a day early and not an hour late. Nothing was left to chance. Everything proceeded according to a divine time schedule. His entire life was pointed toward the precise time of His death.

So it is with each of our lives. There was an appointed time at which we entered this world, and there is an appointed time at which we will depart this world. Nothing can change either date. Knowing that our times are in His hands eliminates needless worry.

HIS RIGHT TO CHOOSE

There is one final dimension of God's sovereignty that the Bible portrays for us. His sovereignty extends to the eternity of His chosen ones, those who in the Bible are called His elect. With unmistakable language, Paul states, "He chose us in Him before the foundation of the world, that we should be holy and blameless before Him" (Ephesians 1:4). Employing similar language, Jesus Himself said, "You did not choose Me, but I chose you" (John 15:16). Not based on any foreseen human faith or good works, God's saving choice is the exercise of *His* own sovereign will. He selects those whom He would save.

Because there are none who seek after God (Romans 3:10–11), God Himself must take the initiative in salvation and choose us, His beloved. In our fallen state, we would never choose Him. The reason we have chosen Him *in* time is because *He* first chose us *before* time. God's sovereignty is seen in the fact that our salvation originates with *His* choice of us, not *our* choice of Him (John 1:13).

Admittedly, this tremendous truth perplexes some and frightens others. In our human thinking, it may even seem unfair. But whatever Scripture affirms, we must embrace. Even with certain questions about God's sovereignty left unanswered, it is not our place to question God's right to choose and do as He pleases. This truth of divine election may run contrary to our human logic, disturb our emotions, and cut against the grain of our democratic mindset, but Scripture nevertheless clearly teaches it. There is nothing unjust about how God exercises His sovereignty (Romans 9:14–24).

At the same time, and paradoxical to our minds, is the truth that although God is fully sovereign, man is completely responsible to believe. One does not negate the other. The greatest of all Baptist preachers, Charles H. Spurgeon, was once asked, "How do you reconcile divine sovereignty with human responsibility?"

Spurgeon replied, "I never have to reconcile friends. Divine sovereignty and human responsibility have never had a falling out with each other. I do not need to reconcile what God has joined together." Neither do we. Both are taught in Scripture, and we must live with the tension.

BEHOLD, YOUR GOD!

In this chapter, we have surveyed the basic realms over which God exercises His sovereignty. We have affirmed His authority over every realm of the universe—over creation, Satan, rulers, nature, circumstances, life, death, and destinies. All these spheres are under our Lord's control.

We must remember that we do not control God, as fans of a user-friendly god would have us believe. It is God who controls us and every aspect of the world in which we live. The user-friendly god has abdicated his right to rule and entrusted man with his sovereignty. But he is a *pitiful* god! Here is a dethroned deity made in man's own image, a product of human imaginations, a god found nowhere in Scripture.

Let us affirm what the Bible declares. God is presently on His throne, ruling and reigning as He pleases, absolutely sovereign in His administration over all the works of creation. In no way relieving man of his responsibility to live by faith and obey the Word, God nevertheless remains the one and only true sovereign over heaven and earth. What we mean is clear and simple—God is *God!*

chapter seven

THE BLACK VELVET BACKDROP

The Wrath of God

—

God's wrath is His righteousness
reacting against unrighteousness.

J. I. PACKER

A young man, planning the moment he would ask the woman he loved to marry him, walked into a jewelry store to shop for an engagement ring. Standing nervously at the counter, he peered through the glass top at a tray of beautiful gems. The salesman brought out some of his finer diamonds to show the hopeful bachelor and held each precious jewel up to the light. The diamonds were quality stones, but the young man was not impressed. None of them caught his eye.

Realizing he needed a new approach, the salesman knew just what to do to get the young man's attention. Wise from his years in the business, the veteran gemologist pulled a black velvet pad out of the drawer and placed it on the counter. Using his tweezers, he delicately picked up one of the choicest stones and laid it on the black backdrop. As he did so, all the light in the room seemed to pour through the stone, causing it to shine as it had never shone before.

The young man was dazzled. He had seen this very same diamond moments earlier, but not like this. All the beauty of this precious stone was now dramatically enhanced and clearly showcased for him to behold. Nodding his approval to the salesman, the young lover said that *this* was the diamond he wanted to purchase. And he did.

What made the difference? Why did the costly gem, which only moments before had appeared so unimpressive, now sparkle like the stars above on a moonless night? What changed the man's view of the diamond?

The black velvet backdrop.

In the jewelry business, the dark background makes all the difference. When placed on a glass counter, the black velvet causes the light overhead to radiate brilliantly through the stone, revealing its true beauty and causing it to sparkle and shine more brightly. Remove the black background, and it is difficult to see the diamond's splendor. It is the darkness that causes the stone to burst forth with dazzling light.

BEAUTY IN THE BLACKNESS

The same principle can be applied to the spiritual realm. In order to fully appreciate God's love and goodness—two attributes of His holy character we will look at in later chapters—we must examine them against the black backdrop of His wrath. Only when we understand that He judges sin—*all* sin, even *our* own sin—can we appreciate His glorious grace for what it is. The darkness of God's wrath showcases the flawless gem of His unmerited mercy toward us. But remove the dark background of His wrath, and our appreciation of the brilliance of His amazing love fades.

The gospel is not good news until we first know the bad news. The good news of His love does not truly become good news until we know the bad news of His wrath. In this chapter we will consider the dark side of God's divine wrath.

NO APOLOGY NEEDED

Tragically though, many Christians today who embrace the user-friendly picture of God regard divine wrath as something for which they need to apologize, if not reject altogether. Many find this truth of divine vengeance distasteful, as though His retribution is somehow unprofitable for discussion or a blemish on His holy character. Some consider God's wrath to be in direct contradiction to His divine love, somehow a violation of His tender mercy. Still others considered it an outmoded, antiquated view of God that has become too unsophisticated for modern man. Therefore, they either leave out the message of divine wrath when they attempt to present the gospel, or they alter it in some fashion to try to make it more appealing to man's "itching ears" (2 Timothy 4:3, NKJV).

In this they are like a jeweler who tries to sell diamonds without using a black backdrop. By offering God's love without mentioning His wrath, they fail in their attempt to genuinely present His grace to lost and dying people. They compromise the Bible's clear teaching on divine vengeance and, in so doing, unknowingly hurt their own cause. By downplaying God's wrath, they inevitably downplay His love. In reality, they have created a god in their own image.

Just as a god without love and mercy is not God, a god without wrath is not God.

In the Bible there is certainly no attempt on God's part to hide the severity of His fierce anger against sin. Like major headlines on the front page of the newspaper that cannot be missed, Scripture refers more to God's wrath than to any other attribute, even His love. These two divine attributes are inextricably linked, and an understanding of His love always requires an understanding of His wrath.

LOVE AND HATE, BALANCE AND BEAUTY

From Genesis to Revelation, the Bible presents a consistent picture of a holy God who reserves wrath for sinners, who is angry with the wicked every day, and yet who, at the same time, loves sinners with the strongest, most tender love.

"How can God be wrathful *and* tenderly loving?" people ask. It seems like a contradiction. But this juxtaposition does not mean that His love negates His holy wrath. Nor does it mean that His grace cancels out the severity of His judgment. Rather, just the opposite is true. His love *necessitates* His wrath. The God who loves righteousness *must* equally hate every form of evil, wherever it is found.

Regarding this balance in God's holy character, the Bible says, "You love righteousness and hate wickedness" (Psalm 45:7). God's wrath is an essential part of His divine nature, a necessary part of His perfect being that fully embraces and magnifies His love. God *must* punish all forms of evil wherever they are found, or His love would be reduced to mere sentimentality, a shallow emotion that is not love at all.

These two divine attributes—wrath and love—in no way contradict, but instead, beautifully complement each other. The apostle Paul invites us to "behold then the kindness and severity of God" (Romans 11:22). God's kindness and severity must be seen together if either one is to be properly understood, appreciated, and even admired. God is perfect in love, yet perfect in wrath. We must always maintain a biblical balance here because a weakening of one will always dilute the other. The Bible says of God:

> A jealous and avenging God is the LORD;
> The LORD is avenging and wrathful.
> The LORD takes vengeance on His adversaries,
> And He reserves wrath for His enemies.
> The LORD is slow to anger and great in power,
> And the LORD will by no means
> leave the guilty unpunished....
> The LORD is good,
> A stronghold in the day of trouble,
> And He knows those who take refuge in Him.
>
> NAHUM 1:2-3, 7

According to this representative passage, God is both consuming and compassionate, both full of fury and filled with forgiveness, both punishing and pardoning.

As those who long to know God, we must understand the depth and breadth of His love. However, before we can, we have to understand what His wrath really is.

WHAT IS GOD'S WRATH?

Simply put, God's wrath is His absolute detestation of all sin and His rightful judgment of it wherever it is found. It is the necessary response of His fierce anger against all that is contrary to His holy nature. It is His expressed displeasure and righteous indignation against all evil. It is the holiness of God stirred into action against sin.

A holy God cannot be indifferent toward the sin that violates His unblemished, pure character. He cannot stand idly by and condone that which rebels against His morally pure nature. He must hate sin. He must judge sinners. Otherwise, He would cease to be holy—which is, of course, impossible.

As His response to sin, God manifests His wrath in five ways—through His cataclysmic wrath, His abandonment wrath, His last days wrath, His eternal wrath, and His redemptive wrath.

CATACLYSMIC WRATH

God's cataclysmic wrath is His righteous anger poured out on sinful humanity in the form of a natural disaster. In the Bible, there are many examples of this manifestation of God's wrath. We see this type of divine vengeance in the universal flood, a devastation that destroyed all forms of life except Noah's immediate family and at least two of every living creature. God unleashed His wrath because of the wickedness in Noah's day. We also see it in the destruction of the pagan peoples who lived in Canaan during the days of Joshua and of foreign armies in the days of Israel's judges and kings.

One example of God's destructive fury was His divine judgment upon Sodom and Gomorrah (Genesis 18–19). Infamous for their gross sins, these two ancient cities had reached a point of no return. Despite Abraham's repeated pleas that God spare them (Genesis 18:22–33), their perversions had become so vile that divine justice *had* to be executed. The behavior of these wicked people had spiraled downward into degrading homosexual relations, an unnatural behavior explicitly forbidden by God.

The situation had become so depraved that when the two angels visited Lot in the city, lustful men asked to have sexual relations with them. This evil enticement prompted them to tell Lot, "We are about to destroy this place, because their outcry has become so great before the LORD that the LORD has sent us to destroy it" (Genesis 19:13). In an act of mercy, God allowed Lot to escape the wicked city. Then He "rained on Sodom and Gomorrah brimstone and fire" (v. 24), wreaking a smoldering vengeance on its carnal citizens.

This is a shocking scene to be sure, for God poured down fire from heaven upon the entire city. Perishing from severe burns is an excruciating way to die, yet this is precisely the punishment God chose to inflict upon a perverted people. Burned to a crisp by the falling fire, they all died.

No Time for Wrath

Despite this biblical account of God's wrath, I frequently hear people speak about God as though He never punishes sin. Many today have adopted the user-friendly god who never judges sinners. Choosing not to entertain frightening thoughts about God's wrath, they favor a feel-good approach to the Almighty.

But this approach indicts God. In a court of law, if a judge knowingly acquits the guilty, he himself becomes corrupt, guilty of the same crime. Along this same line, if God is to be the righteous Judge of heaven and earth, He *must* punish sin, or He Himself would become guilty of it and from moral necessity, topple from His throne of holiness.

The righteous anger of God always burns with indignation against all sin. But those who prefer a user-friendly god don't want it to be like that. I believe that if they could, many people today would label God's fiery display of wrath upon Sodom and Gomorrah as cruel and unusual punishment and demand that heaven make restitution. There are others who believe in God's wrath, but choose never to talk about it or warn lost men and women about it. Their silence is deafening.

Sadly, the modern pulpit has become woefully quiet on the subject of divine retribution. Although some ministers may not fully embrace a user-friendly god, they nevertheless preach as though they do, choosing to talk only about God's love and to say nothing about His wrath.

ABANDONMENT WRATH

As frightful as cataclysmic judgment is, the second type of divine retribution, abandonment wrath, is to be feared even more. This aspect of wrath occurs when God forsakes the one who has repeatedly forsaken Him. According to Scripture, there can come a time when God will remove all restraints against sin in the life of an unbeliever and turn him over to his own sinful desires, allowing him to go his own rebellious way. When this happens, such a person spirals down into the black hole of sin and is never able to find his way back to the light of the knowledge of the truth in order to be saved.

We see the truth of God's abandonment wrath taught throughout the Bible. In the Old Testament, God warned, "Ephraim is joined to idols; Let him alone" (Hosea 4:17). This means that a person can so join himself to another god that the one true God will withdraw His convicting, warning influence, choosing instead to let him alone. God abandons that sinner. This is precisely what God warned about through the psalmist:

> "But My people did not listen to My voice;
> And Israel did not obey Me.
> So I gave them over to the stubbornness of their heart,
> To walk in their own devices."
>
> PSALM 81:11–12

The book of Proverbs issues the same warning. If God's wisdom is repeatedly refused, Solomon says, there may come the time when God will refuse to respond to a plea for help. When He is repeatedly rejected, God may say:

> "Because I called and you refused;
> I stretched out my hand, and no one paid attention;
> And you neglected all my counsel,
> And did not want my reproof; I will even laugh at your calamity;
> I will mock when your dread comes."
>
> PROVERBS 1:24–26

Stated simply, God says that He will abandon those who have abandoned Him.

WHEN GOD GIVES UP

In the New Testament, we find the same expression of abandonment wrath. The apostle Paul writes, "For the wrath of God is revealed from heaven against all ungodliness and unrighteousness of men who suppress the truth in unrighteousness" (Romans 1:18). Notice that this verse speaks of God's wrath in the present tense. This wrath is presently being revealed from heaven against the sin of men.

Paul elaborates upon this wrath: "Therefore God gave them over in the lusts of their hearts to impurity" (Romans 1:24). This wrath occurs when God gives them over to their sins. Advancing this truth further, Paul continues, "For this reason God gave them over to degrading passions; for their women exchanged the natural function for that which is unnatural, and in the same way also the men abandoned the natural function of the woman" (vv. 26–27).

The effects of the abandonment multiplied until finally we read, "God gave them over to a depraved mind, to do those things which are not proper" (v. 28).

Three times in three verses, Paul says that God gives lost men over to their own sinful lusts (vv. 24, 26, 28). By this, he means that God withdraws His restraining influence from their lives and allows them to run after their own sinful desires without any conviction of sin. In fact, He may even cause them to believe a lie because they have so blatantly refused the truth (2 Thessalonians 2:11–12). This abandonment wrath is reserved for the sin of blasphemy against the Holy Spirit, a sin for which there is no forgiveness (Matthew 12:31). This sin occurs when a person rejects God's overtures of grace one time too many and crosses His unseen final deadline, passing the point of no return with God.

We don't hear much today about this aspect of divine wrath. Such a God is offensive to the sophisticated tastes of the modern churchgoer. But this is who God is. Not only is God's wrath being reserved in heaven for the final judgment, it is also being presently revealed in His abandonment of individuals, cultures, and nations who abandon Him. As the prophets declared there is a day when God may be found. We must call upon Him while He is near or be eternally passed by.

LAST-DAYS WRATH

There is yet another aspect of God's wrath—His last-days wrath, which will be poured out on this Christ-rejecting world during the Tribulation, the last hour of this age. The Bible calls this future seven-year period of time "the great day of their wrath" (Revelation 6:17). This climactic outpouring of God's vengeance will be the most perilous time in human history—a time so terrible that those who go through it will hide in caves and say to the mountains, "Fall on us and hide us from the presence of Him who sits on the throne, and from the wrath of the Lamb" (Revelation 6:15–16).

In the Tribulation, God's mounting fury will be unleashed on this sinful planet in unprecedented proportions. From His heavenly throne, Christ will break open the seven-sealed scroll and execute the seven seal judgments—including the coming of the Antichrist, wars, famines, death, martyrdom, and cosmic disturbances (Revelation 6).

This will be a time of unparalleled wrath. When the seventh and final seal judgment is broken open, it will release another seven judgments, known as the seven trumpet judgments (Revelation 8–9). In this outpouring of divine vengeance, the earth, seas, rivers, springs, sun, and moon will all be smitten, sending this planet reeling into convulsions. In addition, the bottomless pit of hell will be opened and a massive hoard of demons will be unleashed to torment and kill men. Literally, all hell will break loose upon the earth.

WRATH UPON WRATH

In potent doses, God will continue to pour out His wrath upon the earth, as the seventh trumpet judgment initiates the seven bowl judgments (Revelation 16). In rapid-fire succession, painful and loathsome sores will inflict sinful people; rivers and seas will turn to blood; the sun will scorch mankind with fire; darkness will cover the earth; and the Euphrates River will be dried up, allowing a massive army from the East to march into the Middle East. Furthermore, the earth will fall prey to lightning, thunder, and earthquakes. As gigantic hailstones pelt the earth, cities will collapse, islands will sink into the sea, and every mountain in the world will be leveled (Revelation 16). God Himself will send all of this!

This future day of wrath will climax in the battle of Armageddon, when God will bring the armies of the world into the Middle East to be utterly destroyed at the return of Christ (Revelation 19). The destruction of human life will be so great that a river of blood will flow as high as a horse's bridle. This sobering display of end-time wrath is reserved for the future, a vengeance presently pent-up, but ready to be revealed in the last days.

As horrible as God's last-days wrath will be, there is another kind of wrath that will surpass it in severity, because it is a wrath that has no end.

ETERNAL WRATH

God's eternal wrath is reserved for all those who reject Christ and who will, consequently, be cast into everlasting hell. This wrath is God's unending punishment that will be unleashed throughout all the ages to come upon Satan, his demons, and lost sinners.

By virtue of God's holiness, hell is just as necessary a reality as heaven. The one without the other would be a gross injustice in the perfect holiness of God. Jesus Christ, who came to seek and save that which is lost, had more to say about hell than anyone else in the Bible.

John the Baptist described hell as "the wrath to come" (Matthew 3:7), a place of "unquenchable fire" (Matthew 3:12). The apostle John taught that hell is the place where lost sinners are "tormented with fire and brimstone" (Revelation 14:10), "the lake of fire" (Revelation 20:15) where the unrepentant are "tormented day and night forever and ever" (Revelation 20:10). The apostle Paul called hell the place where sinners "will pay the penalty of eternal destruction, away from the presence of the Lord" (2 Thessalonians 1:9).

In describing this place called hell, our Lord referred to it by many different names—"fiery hell" (Matthew 5:22), "the furnace of fire" (Matthew 13:42), "the eternal fire" (Matthew 18:8; 25:41), and "where their worm does not die" (Mark 9:48). In addition, Jesus described it as a place of "eternal punishment" (Matthew 25:46), where God will "destroy both soul and body" (Matthew 10:28) and where damned sinners are "in agony in this flame" (Luke 16:24). He also called it "this place of torment" (Luke 16:28).

The effect of this eternal punishment, Jesus said, will be "weeping and gnashing of teeth" (Matthew 8:12), which meant that *all* the weeping that there has ever been in the history of the world— in its wars, disasters, murders, and the like—cannot compare to the weeping of those in hell. The same is true of the gnashing of their teeth, which is the apex of all rage and boiling anger against God Himself, who inflicts His wrath on them there forever.

This eternal wrath in hell will never be extinguished, not in six years, not in sixty years, not in six thousand years, or six million years. *Never* will the flames of God's eternal wrath burn out!

There is one last aspect of divine wrath. It is by far the fiercest, but it is also the one that gives us hope of escaping God's eternal wrath.

REDEMPTIVE WRATH

The Bible teaches that there is a redemptive wrath of God—the wrath poured out upon Christ on the cross. When Jesus died for us, God vented His fury fully upon Him. God made "Him who knew no sin to be sin on our behalf" (2 Corinthians 5:21). Our sin-bearer, Jesus, was also our wrathbearer. A holy God unleashed on Him all the fury of divine anger that we deserved.

In explaining our Lord's death, the prophet Isaiah said:

Surely our griefs He Himself bore,
And our sorrows He carried;
Yet we ourselves esteemed Him stricken,
Smitten of God, and afflicted.

ISAIAH 53:4

Far worse than the physical torment He endured at the hands of the Roman soldiers was the spiritual suffering He endured at the hands of God. The prophet pictures God bruising His own Son, severely inflicting His punishment upon Him as He became sin for us: "But the LORD was pleased to crush Him, putting Him to grief" (v. 10). As Jesus hung suspended in our place, God shot arrow after arrow of His wrath into the bosom of His darling Son.

How real and painful was this wrath? Only those who have died without Christ and now endure God's eternal wrath in hell can even begin to comprehend what Christ endured on our behalf as wave after wave of divine anger washed over His battered soul.

Jesus suffered a wrath equal to the eternal wrath we would suffer forever in hell if we were to die without Him. He who is infinite, the Lord Jesus Christ, suffered in a finite period of time—a few hours upon the cross—what you and I, being finite, would suffer in an infinite period of time in hell. It was as if an eternity in hell were condensed in a limited period of time as He bore for us God's eternal wrath.

If God were ever to withhold His wrath against sin, it would have been in the case of His own Son. But He did not—because all sin *must* be punished! God, who did not spare His Son, will not spare us from being the object of His eternal wrath if we die in our sins. But because God's Lamb bore heaven's wrath for our sins, we need not suffer His vengeance. This is the good news of the gospel. The redemptive wrath of God, unleashed at the cross, means we need not face eternal wrath in hell. When we put our faith in Christ alone, we escape the wrath to come.

God will in one way or the other pour out His wrath on every sin ever committed. Every sin will either be pardoned in Christ or punished in hell.

God is *that* holy.

HOW SHOULD WE RESPOND?

In the light of the truth of God's wrath, how shall we then live? I believe that God's wrath calls for some careful responses.

First, *tremble.* The Bible warns all unbelievers to fear and reverence the Lord: "It is a terrifying thing to fall into the hands of the living God" (Hebrews 10:31). All who are without Christ should tremble before the Lord because it is a fearful thing to appear before His final judgment never having believed in His Son.

If you are unconverted, you have good reason to fear the living God. Jesus said, "Do not be afraid of those who kill the body, and after that have no more that they can do. But I will warn you whom to fear: fear the One who after He has killed has authority to cast into hell; yes, I tell you, fear Him!" (Luke 12:4–5).

Second, *trust.* Because of God's wrath, we must come to Christ and believe in Him, fully relying upon His death to atone for our sins and save us from the wrath to come. Saving faith involves resting completely upon the finished work of Christ to rescue us from God's final judgment.

The Bible asks, "How shall we escape if we neglect so great a salvation...?" (Hebrews 2:3). The unstated answer to this question is that there is no deliverance from God's final, eternal wrath if we do not believe in Christ. In the truest sense of the word, He is the Savior come to rescue us from the eternal punishment of hell. Only by trusting in Christ alone for the forgiveness of our sins can we be saved and be made right before God.

Third, *thanksgiving*. After we believe in Him and receive His salvation, gratitude should flood our hearts because we have been delivered from the wrath to come. David cried out:

> Bless the LORD, O my soul,
> And all that is within me, bless His holy name!
>
> PSALM 103:1

Why should we offer praise and thanksgiving? Because, David says, God is the God "who pardons all your iniquities" (v. 3). "He has not dealt with us according to our sins, nor rewarded us according to our iniquities" (v.10).

A thankful spirit should grip our hearts every moment of every day because we are eternally saved. No matter what trials may come our way in the circumstances of life, we have *every* reason to be thankful, because His redemptive wrath has spared us from His eternal wrath.

Nevertheless, let us not minimize the reality—and the darkness—of God's wrath. The darker, the better! It is His divine anger that causes our once-calloused hearts to tremble, leading us to trust in Christ's grace and receive "so great a salvation."

All of this leads to the subject of God's love.

Keep reading.

chapter eight

THE MOST PROFOUND TRUTH EVER KNOWN

The Love of God

—

God does not love us because we
are valuable, but we are valuable
because God loves us.
MARTIN LUTHER

Several years before his death, the noted Swiss theologian Karl Barth came to the United States for a series of lectures. While speaking at the Harvard Divinity School, the venerable scholar agreed to a question and answer session with the entire student body.

The lecture hall was jammed with young students of theology. After Barth's presentation, the floor was opened to questions, and a young student asked, "Dr. Barth, what is the greatest thought that has ever passed through your mind?"

With that pointed query, every student in the lecture hall leaned forward, awaiting the reply of the aged professor. It was as though Einstein had been asked to explain the theory of relativity.

Everyone expected some complicated and incomprehensible answer.

After he thought for what seemed to be a long time, Barth replied, "The deepest truth to ever enter my mind is this: Jesus loves me, this I know. For the Bible tells me so."

GOD'S LOVE: THE MYSTERY OF ALL MYSTERIES

Barth was correct about God's love being a deep and profound truth. It is an infinite mystery that God has chosen to love us, unworthy sinners that we are, and deliver us from certain judgment. In the greatest display of love ever known, God gave His Son, Jesus Christ, to die voluntarily for the sins of people who were His enemies. Referring to a world in rebellion against God, John records this monumental truth in the words of Christ Himself: "God so loved the world, that He gave His only begotten Son, that whoever believes in Him should not perish, but have eternal life" (John 3:16).

The fact that God loves undeserving sinners like you and me is the mystery of all mysteries. Certainly, it is not inconceivable that we should love Him, given the fact that He is so great and glorious. But that He, the great God of heaven and earth, should love us—unworthy sinners that we are—now *that* is truly amazing!

NOW FOR THE GOOD NEWS

You may be asking: If God's love is so great, why have we postponed our discussion of it until now? Why did we not begin this book with a survey of His love?

It is simple. Before we could appreciate the riches of God's love, we first had to see the humbling depravity of the sin that separates us from a holy God. Only after we see the depths of His righteous wrath can we appreciate the heights of His unmerited love. If, however, we were to rearrange the sequence of thought and speak first of God's love, with no understanding of His holiness, we would minimize His love and not treasure it as we should. In our minds it would be nothing like the holy love we see in the Bible.

Only after we comprehend the bad news does the Good News truly become good news.

USER-FRIENDLY MUSH

Whenever we elevate God's love to a preeminent place in our thinking without first considering His holiness, sovereignty, and wrath, we distort the true picture of God. We reduce His love to syrupy, sentimental mush and turn Him into a user-friendly god who pats us on the head instead of delivering us from condemnation.

This god loves sinners—as God does—but his holiness, sovereignty, and wrath are downplayed, if not altogether denied. Consequently, we may understand that we are saved, but we don't know *from what* we are saved—namely, God's anger at our sin and eternal separation from Him in a place described in the Bible as the lake of fire and brimstone. At best, he is a god who can save us from temporal problems such as loneliness, anxiety, apathy, and aimlessness, but not from the power and eternal penalty of sin.

To make matters worse, today's secular music, movies, and other media have greatly shaped our thoughts of what love is all about. Stripped of its true meaning, love is most often presented as mere romantic feelings, or even as illicit lustful desires. We are bombarded with talk of puppy love, falling in love, falling out of love, making love, free love, and so on. From songs of the music industry to frivolous valentine cards at the mall, the meaning of love has been so diluted that it in no way resembles divine love. Sad to say, much of this drivel has become part of our thinking about God's love. The result is a distorted understanding of God's love that is nothing more than user-friendly mush.

This feel-good message has become the predominant message in many churches today. In an effort not to offend people or make them uncomfortable, preachers do not tell seekers about God's holiness and wrath. But ignoring this part of God's character diminishes the message of divine acceptance. In extending the free offer of the gospel, the user-friendly god makes few or no demands. The user-friendly gospel doesn't require self-examination, repentance, or obedience. Instead, there is talk only of a "loving" god who accepts people just as they are without requiring any commitment or change. In this scenario, God's love is equated with accepting us, condoning our sins, and excusing our offenses.

Is it any wonder that our thoughts of God's love are at an all-time low?

HEREIN IS LOVE

There is nothing soft, passive, or mushy about God's love. In fact, His love is so strong that He committed Himself to save us while we were still His enemies, and He decisively intervened to deliver us from His own wrath.

Having considered the black velvet backdrop of His wrath, we can now truly appreciate the priceless gem of His infinite love. With the necessary foundation firmly laid, let us consider the fullness of His love for us.

As you read on, you will see just how amazing God's love for us really is.

LOVING THE UNLOVELY

If we are to rightly understand God's love, we must comprehend the fact that God has chosen to love those who are under His wrath. In other words, we do not *deserve* God's love. There is nothing in us to attract or prompt His love. He chooses to love us simply because He *is* love. Sin had ruined our lives. God loved us in spite of ourselves, not because of ourselves.

Commenting on God's gracious love, the apostle Paul wrote, "But God demonstrates His own love toward us, in that while we were yet sinners, Christ died for us" (Romans 5:8). This is what we were when God exercised His great love toward us—*sinners*. In fact, Paul identifies us as "enemies" of God (v. 10). In other words, we were living in a state of self-declared war against Him. And to make matters worse, He was at war with us. Yet, it was when we were hostile foes and bitter adversaries that God chose to love us.

Describing just how unlovely we were when God loved us, the apostle Paul wrote:

> You were dead in your trespasses and sins,
> in which you formerly walked according
> to the course of this world, according to
> the prince of the power of the air,
> of the spirit that is now working
> in the sons of disobedience.
>
> EPHESIANS 2:1–2

Like dead fish floating downstream in the polluted waters of this world's corrupt system, we were nothing more than spiritual corpses, following the devil and living a lifestyle of disobedience to God.

Yet despite our wickedness and depravity, God chose to love us. Paul wrote: "But God, being rich in mercy, because of His great love with which He loved us, even when we were dead in our transgressions, made us alive together with Christ" (Ephesians 2:4–5). The apostle John pointed out that God chose to love us simply because He is love (1 John 4:8–9).

He Loved Us First

God's love is an *initiating* love. He is *always* the pursuer in loving us, never the responder.

We could easily understand God's reaching out to love those who first loved Him. Limited by our human nature, we think that is the way love operates. We are drawn to love people who are nice and considerate toward us. But not God! He loves those who do not love Him and who are, in fact, hostile toward Him.

How incomprehensible to us is the idea of extending love to an enemy! But that is precisely how God has exercised His love toward us. In the midst of our rebellion against Him, God took the initiative to reach out and love us, long before we ever loved Him. "We love, because He first loved us," the apostle John wrote (1 John 4:19). This clearly states that God's love sought us out even when we were not interested in Him.

God's love is a totally different kind of love. "See how great a love the Father has bestowed upon us," wrote John (1 John 3:1). "How great a love" means that His love is completely foreign to the love that we naturally show each other. It is an out-of-this-world kind of love.

He Holds Nothing Back

By its very nature God's love is a *sacrificial* love, meaning that instead of giving us what we deserve—His wrath—God has sacrificially given us what we do not deserve but so desperately need—

His grace. Despite the fact that we were condemned sinners, justly under His wrath, God lavished His love upon us in the gift of His Son, Jesus Christ. This is the heart of what the apostle Paul writes in Galatians 4:4: "But when the fullness of the time came, God sent forth His Son, born of a woman, born under the Law."

Jesus is the best God had to give for there is no one who can compare with God's Son. Giving the greatest gift ever given, God the Father lavished His infinite, limitless love on us by giving His only Son. John writes, "By this the love of God was manifested in us, that God has sent His only begotten Son into the world so that we might live through Him" (1 John 4:9). God's amazing love is documented in His giving His Son to die for us.

While His love is free to us, it is certainly not cheap. It came at an infinite cost to God, who sacrificially gave what was most valuable to Him, His only Son.

FREE, BUT NOT CHEAP

A soldier once approached the great British preacher G. Campbell Morgan, pastor of Westminster Chapel in London, and said he would give anything to believe that God would forgive sins.

"I cannot believe He will forgive me if I just turn to Him," he said. "That's too cheap."

Dr. Morgan said to him, "You were working in the mine today. How did you get out of the pit?"

The man answered, "The way I usually do. I got into the cage and was pulled to the top."

"How much did you pay to come out of the pit?"

"I didn't pay anything," he replied.

"Weren't you afraid to trust yourself to that cage? Was it not too cheap?"

The man replied, "Oh no! It was cheap for me, but it cost the company a lot of money to sink that shaft."

With that answer, the man saw the light. In a moment, he understood what it had cost God to secure our salvation—the death of His Son. God's love is offered freely, but it is anything but cheap.

Unmistakably, *this* is love. Here is God providing salvation without cost to guilty sinners, paying the ultimate price to seek His ultimate glory—the salvation of man. Even the angels wonder at this amazing love (1 Peter 1:12). And all this is offered to us as a free, prepaid gift.

LOVE THAT TRANSCENDS TIME

What I find even more remarkable about God's love is that it is *eternal*. Rising above the confines of time, it reaches back to eternity past and stretches forward to eternity future. Before time began, before we ever could have loved Him, God initiated His love for us.

"He chose us in Him before the foundation of the world," Paul wrote, "that we should be holy and blameless before Him. In love He predestined us to adoption as sons through Jesus Christ to Himself" (Ephesians 1:4–5). According to this passage, God's love for us welled up before the creation of the world. "I have loved you with an everlasting love; therefore I have drawn you with lovingkindness," He said through the prophet Jeremiah (Jeremiah 31:3). Before God created heaven and earth, He loved us in Christ and set His heart upon us.

Furthermore, God's love will endure throughout eternity future. Even in the ages to come, nothing will hinder the flow of God's perfect love toward us in Christ. Far different from the world's kind of love, which is fickle and frail, God's love remains steadfast and stable forever. No fewer than twenty-six times in Psalm 136, once in each verse, the psalmist wrote, "His lovingkindness is everlasting." While the everlasting nature of His love is hard to comprehend, it is not hard to appreciate and enjoy. God's deep, abiding love for us, His people, will never be exhausted. His lovingkindness, the psalmist exulted, is *everlasting!*

The apostle Paul emphasized this truth when he wrote:

> Neither death, nor life, nor angels, nor principalities,
> nor things present, nor things to come,
> nor powers, nor height, nor depth,
> nor any other created thing,
> will be able to separate us from the love of God,
> which is in Christ Jesus our Lord.
>
> ROMANS 8:38–39

God's eternal love will *never* end but will triumphantly endure forever. God, and God alone, loves with such unfailing love.

HIS LOVE WILL NEVER CHANGE

God's love is *immutable.* This means that just as God Himself is unchanging, so is His love toward us. Leaving no room for misunderstanding, He declares, "For I, the LORD, do not change; therefore you, O sons of Jacob, are not consumed" (Malachi 3:6). By this He means that His unchangeable character causes Him to remain constant in His love toward us, restraining His wrath even when we deserve to be consumed by it. Such steadfast love is fixed, based on His once-for-all-time, settled commitment toward us. It *cannot* change.

Because God's love is immutable, it can neither increase nor decrease. It certainly cannot grow stronger, because that would mean it is now less than perfect. Neither can it diminish, because that would mean it would become less than perfect.

There is nothing we can do that will cause God to love us more, nor is there anything we can do to prompt Him to love us less. Such constant love precludes self-imposed, legalistic thinking whereby we would wrongly assume that any good works on our part could alter God's love for us. God wants a relationship with us, not a performance from us. He does not love us more when we please Him, nor does He love us less when we displease Him. Instead, with a constant, fixed love in Christ, He forever loves us the same yesterday, today, and forever.

WINNING OUR HEARTS

Because God is a powerful God, His love is a *powerful* love. As God extends His grace to us, He overcomes our stubborn hearts and draws us to Himself. Although we refused His love when He first extended it to us, He continued to pursue us until He finally conquered our proud hearts.

Describing this glorious power, Jesus said, "No one can come to Me, unless the Father who sent Me draws him" (John 6:44). The Father's powerful love is seen in His effectual drawing to personal faith in Christ all those He had given to the Son (John 6:37). This word *drawing* is the Greek word used in John 21:11: Peter "drew the net to land, full of large fish." Just as Peter powerfully pulled in his catch of fish with his burly, strong arms, so the strong arm of God the Father draws us to Christ by the omnipotent work of the Holy Spirit, who compels our hearts to believe the gospel.

The Bible tells us that the sin of unbelief is so strong that no one *can* come to Christ by his or her own impulse (Romans

3:10–12). Only a greater power—God's triumphant love—can soften the hardness of our hearts and bring us to believe in Christ.

Though we initially resisted Him, God's love prevailed over our proud hearts and brought us into a relationship with Him through faith in Christ. Once enslaved to sin and unable to come to Christ, we were enabled to believe in Him by divine empowering. Now, *that* is powerful love!

LOVE BEYOND COMPREHENSION

Love like God's toward us is beyond our capacity to understand. It is an incomprehensible love that far outweighs any human love we will ever know, and it surpasses any earthly knowledge we will attain.

The apostle Paul prayed that the believers at Ephesus would "be able to comprehend with all the saints what is the breadth and length and height and depth, and to know the love of Christ which surpasses knowledge," so that they might be "filled up to all the fullness of God" (Ephesians 3:18–19). Paradoxically, Paul prayed that they might know the unknowable. This was his way of emphasizing that he wanted them to enter more deeply into the vastness of God's infinite love, one that far exceeds human reason and experience. Only God Himself, Paul stated, can open our eyes to see even the surface of the deep, fathomless riches of His amazing love for us (Ephesians 1:17–18).

Declaring this same truth through the prophet Isaiah, God said that His love is far beyond the human ability to understand:

> "For My thoughts are not your thoughts,
> Nor are your ways My ways," says the LORD.

"For as the heavens are higher than the earth,
So are My ways higher than your ways,
And My thoughts than your thoughts."

ISAIAH 55:8–9, NKJV

This means we cannot fully comprehend the infinite love God has for us.

THERE'S NOTHING GREATER!

Peter Miller, a faithful preacher during the Revolutionary War, lived near a man who hated him intensely because of his Christian life and testimony. In fact, the man violently opposed Miller and sought to do him great harm.

One day this unbeliever was found guilty of treason and was sentenced to death. Upon hearing this, Miller set out on foot to meet with George Washington to intercede on behalf of the man and plead for his life. The general listened to the minister's earnest plea but told him he did not believe he should pardon his friend.

"My *friend?* He is not my friend," answered Miller. "In fact, he's my worst enemy."

"What?" said Washington. "You have walked sixty miles to save the life of your enemy? That, in my judgment, puts the matter in a different light. I will grant your request."

With pardon in hand, Miller hastened to the place where his adversary was to be executed, arriving just as the condemned prisoner was walking to the scaffold to be hanged. When the traitor saw Miller, he exclaimed with bitter anger, "Old Peter Miller has come to seek his revenge by watching me hang!" But to his astonishment, he watched the minister step out of the crowd and produce the pardon that spared his life.

Peter Miller demonstrated a very uncommon love, something that is to be highly commended. But as great as it was, Miller's gesture is merely a shadow of the love God has shown us in Jesus Christ. Far more serious than the death sentence of Miller's protagonist was our state of eternal condemnation before God.

While we were yet sinners, Christ died for us. Although far beyond our human ability to grasp, the truth is that God *has* chosen to love us in Christ. While we were His enemies at war against His throne through our defiant disobedience, God initiated His unconditional love for us. Reaching out to save us, undeserving, guilty people that we were, God gave His Son to die for our sins so that we could be reconciled to Him and spend all eternity with Him in heaven as His adopted children.

God's love—this *is* the greatest truth ever known.

chapter nine

PURSUED BY HIS MERCY

The Goodness of God

—

God's goodness is the root of all
goodness; and our goodness, if we
have any, springs out of his goodness.
WILLIAM TYNDALE

D r. Harry Ironside, one of the great Bible teachers of the first half of the twentieth century, spent many years of fruitful ministry pastoring the Moody Memorial Church in downtown Chicago. During that time, many people came to him for counseling and spiritual help, among them a woman who was deeply distraught.

The source of the woman's problem, she told Ironside, was that two men followed her wherever she went. Whenever she got on the bus to ride downtown, these two strangers trailed her, boarding directly behind her. When she got off the bus, they disembarked, always staying close behind her. In fact, she continued, they were right outside the pastor's office now, waiting for her to leave.

"What should I do?" she asked with a nervous twitch and darting eyes.

It did not take Ironside long to detect that this dear woman was not emotionally stable. It was obvious that the two pursuing men were figments of her imagination. Wanting to comfort her troubled heart, he replied, "I know who they are. As a matter of fact, I know them by name."

"You do?" she replied with amazement. "Who are they?"

"Those are two of King David's friends," he said. "David told us about his two accomplices in Psalm 23. Let me introduce you to them."

With that, Ironside opened his Bible to the twenty-third Psalm and read verse 6: "Surely goodness and mercy shall follow me all the days of my life; and I will dwell in the house of the LORD forever."

Looking up at her, he said, "Those men who are following you are David's two friends whom he has sent to comfort you wherever you go. The Bible says their names are Goodness and Mercy, and they will always be with you to help in time of need."

"Oh," she said, "that's wonderful! I will make certain to thank them when I leave."

SHADOWING OUR STEPS

Are we as trusting of God's Word as that dear woman who came to Pastor Ironside? Do we believe God's Word for what it truly says? His goodness and mercy—not fictitious characters, but the constant presence of God's care—*do* follow us wherever we go. All the days of our lives, God's amazing love stalks us, shadowing our steps in our every endeavor. God is abundantly good to us, and He delights in constantly pouring His superabundant mercy upon us.

God's goodness begins with His own character. Our word for Lord—"God"—is derived from the German word for *good*. God is so good that our most common name for Him literally means good. His is the highest good in the entire universe and the source of all goodness. Everything about God—His heart, His thoughts, His motives, His choices—is good! He cannot be anything but good.

God summarized each successive day of creation by saying that it was *good* (Genesis 1:4, 10, 12, 18, 21, 25). In fact, after He made everything, He concluded that it was *very good* (v. 31). "Good and upright is the LORD," David declared (Psalm 25:8). This means that God is good, and therefore, all that He does is devoid of any evil or wrong.

The prophet Nahum concurred:

> The LORD is good, a stronghold in the day of trouble,
> And He knows those who take refuge in Him.
>
> NAHUM 1:7

God *does* good because He *is* good. He is a virtual storehouse of goodness for all who trust Him.

A NOT-SO-GOOD GOD?

Despite the goodness of God, I frequently hear people say the very opposite about Him. Many people look at the world and wrongly conclude that God is not so good. Hurricanes in Honduras, earthquakes in Turkey, ethnic cleansing in Bosnia, starving children in Africa, and school shootings in America convince them that God is uncaring, capricious, and indifferent. "How could a good God allow such suffering?" they ask.

Doubting God's goodness, they surmise that He is powerful enough to stop human suffering around the globe but not caring enough to intervene and prevent it from occurring. In their hearts and minds, they create a counterfeit god, one who is not good or kind. Their god, made in their own image, is less than perfectly good.

Others assume that God is not good. They think that He is a stoic sovereign who runs the universe with robotic dispassion or that He controls the world as one would play a chess match—emotionally detached in His heart from each of the pieces on the board. They think of Him as aloof, distanced, cerebral, and uncaring toward the individuals He made in His image. They liken Him to a utilitarian general who has to make decisions for the greater good of the war effort without any concern for the nameless individuals lost in battle. As He presides over the affairs of this world, He may be working for good on the larger scale, but not for the good of each individual.

Because bad things sometimes happen to good people, many people conclude that God must not be good. Such reasoning distorts their perspective of reality because they assume that man is good and God is bad. In first doubting God's goodness, then outright denying it, they replace the true God with an imaginary deity of their own making.

Theirs is not the true picture of God—it's not even close!

GOD IS GOOD, ALL THE TIME!

As with all His divine attributes, God's goodness is unlimited and far exceeds all comparisons. The Bible declares, "How great is Your goodness" (Psalm 31:19, NKJV). This means that God's goodness must be extraordinary in its measure.

God's goodness is so great that the Bible declares, "the earth is full of the goodness of the LORD" (Psalm 33:5, NKJV). The psalmist wrote, "The goodness of God endures continually" (Psalm 52:1,

NKJV). This means that His goodness will never cease to flow into our lives. Day by day there is a continual supply of His goodness in all that we do. The psalmist also said, "We shall be satisfied with the goodness of Your house, of Your holy temple" (Psalm 65:4, NKJV).

Notice, moreover, that God is so good that whenever we come into His presence, we are coming into His goodness. God and His goodness are inseparably linked! Describing worshipers approaching God's house, the prophet declared:

"They shall come and sing in the height of Zion,
Streaming to the goodness of the LORD"
JEREMIAH 31:12, NKJV

All who come before the Lord will be made glad because they are actually drawing near to His goodness.

Pointing to "the riches of His goodness" (Romans 2:4, NKJV), the apostle Paul exulted in God's goodness, calling upon all men to repent and trust in this good God. How could anyone resist such a good God, a God who is so full of kindness toward us? Only in living and walking in His goodness are our hearts truly satisfied.

There are many facets of God's goodness. As we trace these streams of mercy that flow from His throne, we will discover six major tributaries that pour forth His goodness into our lives: His plans, His providence, His provision, His protection, His patience, and His pardon.

HIS PLANS ARE GOOD

First, the Bible teaches that God is good in His plans for us. For example, Paul wrote that God's will is "good and acceptable and perfect" (Romans 12:2, NKJV). Since God's plan for us as individuals is good, it is not to be feared or avoided, but embraced. As a perfect reflection of His own holy character, God's will is good because God Himself is good.

God allowed disobedient Israel to be carried away into captivity. Still, He declared: "I know the plans that I have for you...plans for welfare and not for calamity to give you a future and a hope" (Jeremiah 29:11). God assured His people that, despite all appearances to the contrary, His plans for them remained infinitely good. It was the kind intention of God's heart to give them a future and a hope despite their present, self-inflicted trial. God was too good not to work for their welfare!

The same is true for our lives. When we disobey God, we too invite adversity; nevertheless, God's plans for tomorrow remain good. God's perfect will includes the good works He has planned for us to accomplish. Paul wrote, "For we are His workmanship, created in Christ Jesus for good works, which God prepared beforehand, that we should walk in them" (Ephesians 2:10). In the same way He planned our salvation before time began. God has eternally purposed good things for us to do. Thus there is a real sense of destiny about our daily lives. From before the foundation of the world, God has gone before us into the future and planned good works for us to do, a wonderful expression of His own goodness toward us.

God has not planned for us to live mundane, meaningless lives. Not only has He planned the end of our salvation—glorification—He has also graciously designed the means to that end, our sanctification and good works according to His will.

HIS PROVIDENCE IS GOOD

Second, not only does God plan good things for us, He also sovereignly works to bring these good things to pass. The divine certainty by which He guarantees that these preordained things will be realized in our lives is called His providence. *Providence* is a theological term that refers to the loving, sovereign care with which God governs all the affairs and circumstances of our daily lives.

Addressing this truth, the apostle Paul said, "And we know that God causes all things to work together for good to those who love God, to those who are called according to His purpose" (Romans 8:28). According to this verse, God micromanages all that occurs in our lives to bring about good for us. With perfect design and infinite wisdom, God coordinates every event and occurrence in our lives—our triumphs and tragedies and everything in between—for the highest good, which He defines as being "conformed to the image of His Son" (v. 29).

What an expression of His goodness toward us!

This does not mean that God will not allow evil to occur in our lives. It means that He will use even the evil for our good. The Bible teaches that because God is good, He will use for our good even that which others mean for our harm.

The much-loved story of Joseph is a classic example of this truth. Sold into slavery by his jealous brothers, falsely accused by Potiphar's wife, and wrongly imprisoned in Egypt, Joseph nevertheless kept sight of the fact that God was at work for his good. Despite these setbacks, many years later Joseph confidently told his brothers, "You meant evil against me, but God meant it for good" (Genesis 50:20).

There is no clearer illustration of God's benevolent providence over the affairs of men than the death of Jesus Christ. The Cross is the ultimate example of God providentially using sinful, sinister powers to accomplish His good pleasure. Although the Pharisees conspired against and falsely accused Jesus, Judas betrayed Him, the Romans declared Him guilty, and godless men murdered Him on the cross, Jesus remained submitted to the will of God the Father. In the face of evil forces, dead religion, and painful adversity, God sovereignly worked out our highest good—eternal salvation.

Perhaps you have been the victim of some great evil. Perhaps you have greatly suffered because of the sinful actions of another. If so, I want you to know that God is so good that He can use even the great harm that has fallen upon you for your spiritual good. Because His goodness is inseparable from His sovereignty and His wisdom, He can use evil to carry out His eternal purposes for your life. Although your experience has doubtless been painful and confusing, be assured of God's perfect goodness toward you. He will use the evil done to you for your good—to conform you to the image of Christ.

HIS PROVISION IS GOOD

Third, God is also the giver of all good things in our lives. The Scripture tells us, "Every good thing bestowed and every perfect gift is from above, coming down from the Father of lights, with whom there is no variation, or shifting shadow" (James 1:17). This means that everything good in our lives comes from God. The absolute goodness of God results in His giving good gifts to us. Our loving heavenly Father cannot give bad or evil gifts to His children.

Jesus said that God provides good things for His children in response to their prayers. Using imagery with which people could identify, Christ asked:

> "What man is there among you who, if his son
> ask for bread, will give him a stone?
> Or if he asks for a fish, will he give him a serpent?
> If you then, being evil, know how to give good gifts

to your children, how much more will your Father
who is in heaven give good things to those who ask Him!"
MATTHEW 7:9–11, NKJV

If men plagued with human depravity give good gifts to their children, how much more will our holy, perfect Father give us what is good! Just as it is in the heart of an earthly father to provide good things for his children, so it is God's loving desire to provide good things for us. God will withhold nothing good from us, whether it comes in this life or in the one to come.

The apostle Paul wrote, "He who did not spare His own Son, but delivered Him up for us all, how will He not also with Him freely give us all things?" (Romans 8:32). If God gave us the greatest gift, Jesus Christ, while we were still His enemies, will He not give us other good gifts pertaining to daily living now that we are His children? This rhetorical question demands an unequivocal yes!

God's goodness toward us is unrestrained, abounding in good gifts. Psalm 84:11 says:

> For the LORD God is a sun and shield;
> The LORD gives grace and glory;
> No good thing does He withhold
> from those who walk uprightly.

David said, "They who seek the LORD shall not be in want of any good thing" (Psalm 34:10). God is so good that He delights in providing for our needs.

God is so good that He provides for those no one else cares for—the poor. David exulted, "You, O God, provided from Your goodness for the poor" (Psalm 68:10). God gives good things to those from whom men withhold good. People may not notice the poor, but God does. He cares for all because He is rich in goodness.

God is so good that He even provides for the general welfare of His enemies. Jesus Himself said, "He causes His sun to rise on the evil and the good, and sends rain on the righteous and the unrighteous" (Matthew 5:45). God indiscriminately showers His blessings on all, unbeliever and believer alike.

HIS PROTECTION IS GOOD

Fourth, God expresses His kindness through the protection He provides for His own. An earthly father who loves his children wants to protect them. Infinitely greater than that of a human father is God's protection of His own children. With omnipotent might and wise intervention, God shields us from all that would harm us.

This doesn't necessarily mean God will keep us from all danger, but we know from reading His Word that He will safely preserve us in the midst of our trials and keep us from anything that will not work for our ultimate good. As a loving Father, God knows what we can handle without failing. Therefore, He promises that He will never allow us to be tempted beyond what we can endure (1 Corinthians 10:13). Nothing comes into our lives that has not first passed through His hands.

With words of strong encouragement, the prophet reminds us:

> The LORD is good,
> A stronghold in the day of trouble,
> And He knows those who take refuge in Him.
>
> NAHUM 1:7

In this verse, one that we considered earlier, God's goodness is pictured as an unshakable refuge that protects us from harm when we run to Him with humble trust in our times of adversity. He is our unassailable tower, a mighty fortress to all who rely on Him, a shield of protection in the midst of threatening storms (Psalm 18:1–2).

Do you find yourself in a time of trouble? Are you presently in the midst of a turbulent storm of life? Know that God is your ever-present stronghold, able to protect you from all that would harm you. As you put your trust in Him, you will find His loving arms around you, shielding you from the harmful forces that otherwise would crush you.

HIS PATIENCE IS GOOD

Fifth, God reveals His goodness in His patience toward us when we sin and fail Him. As much as we may deserve God's immediate rebuke or discipline, God is not quick to anger. Instead He is amazingly longsuffering toward us. Identifying Himself as "the LORD God, merciful and gracious, longsuffering, and abounding in goodness and truth" (Exodus 34:6, NKJV), God reveals Himself as one who deals patiently with us. The word *long-suffering* describes someone who has the power to avenge but doesn't. Though we may deserve it, God withholds His punishment from us for long periods of time because He is long-suffering.

Boasting of God's goodness, the psalmist declared:

> The LORD is compassionate and gracious,
> Slow to anger and abounding in lovingkindness.
>
> PSALM 103:8

This means that God does not fly off the handle when provoked. Rather, He is so full of goodness that He patiently gives us time to repent before He responds. "The Lord is not slow about His promise, as some count slowness," wrote the apostle Peter, "but is patient toward you, not wishing for any to perish but for all to come to repentance" (2 Peter 3:9).

Even within the purview of His sovereignty, God is so good that He delays judgment and patiently allows sinners time to come to Him and be saved.

HIS PARDON IS GOOD

Finally, God's goodness is seen in His pardoning our sins. There is no greater danger from which we have been delivered than the just consequences of our sins, and there is no greater blessing that we may receive than His forgiveness. Therefore, there is no greater expression of God's goodness than His forgiveness of undeserving sinners like you and me.

One man who learned the goodness of God's forgiveness was King David, who wrote:

> For You, LORD, are good, and ready to forgive,
> And abundant in mercy to all those who call upon You.
> PSALM 86:5, NKJV

David had committed adultery and murder (2 Samuel 11–12). As great as these sins were, the goodness of God's forgiveness was greater still. Although David turned his back on the Lord by choosing to sin against Him, God nevertheless showered him with divine goodness in the form of abundant pardon for his sin when he confessed it. God is good, the psalmist said, because He is ready to forgive all who call on Him.

We need to remind ourselves that out of His goodness God

readily forgives us when we turn to Him in humble repentance, confessing our sins. This is precisely what the Bible teaches when it says, "If we confess our sins, He is faithful and righteous to forgive us our sins and to cleanse us from all unrighteousness" (1 John 1:9). God is not reluctant to pardon us, but is eager to wash away our iniquities. Instead of nursing a grudge, God is ready to start anew in His dealings with us. He convicts us of our sin so that we will draw near to Him, confess it, and be forgiven.

After the apostle Peter had shamefully denied Him, Jesus took the initiative to rebuild their fractured relationship. He sought out this disobedient disciple and asked him three times, "Simon, son of John, do you love Me?" (John 21:15–17). This gentle correction restored Peter to full usefulness in His work.

The psalmist could not contain himself when he rejoiced in the goodness of God's pardon.

> Blessed is he whose transgression is forgiven,
> Whose sin is covered!
> How blessed is the man to whom the LORD
> does not impute iniquity,
> And in whose spirit there is no deceit!
> PSALM 32:1–2

David had lived with his sin for an entire year; but when he finally confessed it to God, he found immediate forgiveness, prompting him to extol God's forgiveness. May we be quick to confess our sins, knowing that God is quick to forgive us when we do. He is good to all who call upon Him.

GREAT IN HIS GOODNESS

Having reflected upon God's goodness, we can only conclude that it is so vast that it cannot be contained or restrained. As the ultimate source of all goodness, God is good in His plans, providence, provision, protection, patience, and pardon. There is no good in our lives that did not come directly from God. As a good heavenly Father, His very nature is to shower His goodness on us.

People who serve a user-friendly god, however, minimize God's goodness, because they deny that everything good in our lives has come from God. This self-made deity, one shaped in our own image, is the source of some good, they say, but one who also gives man some credit for being good. This is *not* the God of the Bible. Concerning the goodness of man, the Bible says, "There is none who does good, no, not one" (Romans 3:12, NKJV).

God has revealed Himself in the Scriptures as the *only* source of good, the gracious provider for His people and the fulfiller of all our needs, who alone causes all things to work together for our good. As Jesus said to the rich young ruler, "No one is good except God alone" (Luke 18:19).

Wherever we go, whatever we do, may the words of the twenty-third Psalm reverberate in our hearts. Despite how things may appear in this life, God's goodness toward us who love Him never changes. Surely His goodness will follow us all the days of our life. And when we die, we will dwell in the house of the Lord forever, there to enjoy the full measure of His perfect goodness toward us.

As we come to know the true God, may we grow to know the richness of His goodness.

chapter ten

ONLY GOD
IS GREAT!

The Glory of God

—

*Glory is essential to the Godhead,
as light is to the sun.
Glory is the sparkling of the Deity.*
THOMAS WATSON

A scending the throne at age four, Louis XIV ruled as king of France for seventy-two years, the longest reign in modern European history. Consumed with his own power, he called himself the "Great Monarch" and declared, "I am the State!" But in 1715, King Louis XIV abdicated his throne to death.

His funeral was nothing short of spectacular. The great cathedral was packed with mourners paying final tribute to their king, who lay in a solid gold coffin. To dramatize the deceased ruler's greatness, a solitary candle burned above his coffin. Thousands waited in hushed silence as they peered at the exquisite casket that held the mortal remains of their monarch.

At the appointed time the funeral service began, and Bishop Massillon, who presided over this official act of state, stood to address the mourners, including the assembled clergy of France. When the bishop rose, he did something that stunned the nation.

Bending down from the pulpit, he snuffed out the lone candle representing Louis XIV's greatness. The people gasped. Then, in the darkness, came just four words from behind the open Bible:

"Only God is great!"

GOD AND GOD ALONE

The message of this story—only God is great—is a much-needed reminder at a time when people have man-centered views of God. We must be people who champion the greatness of God because He, as Scripture affirms, will not share His glory with another.

A. W. Tozer once said, "God is looking for men in whose hands His glory is safe." By this, he meant that God uses only people who have a high view of who He is and who are jealous for the honor of His holy name. God is searching for men and women who will lay down their own glory before His throne and give Him the glory He alone deserves. He is looking for people who are absorbed in His surpassing glory and who are jealous for His name, not theirs.

Unfortunately, the glory of God has fallen on hard times. The user-friendly god has diminished what Tozer called the "Godhead of God" and compromised the picture of the wonder and glory of God's holy attributes. Many people, even in evangelical circles, have adopted a man-centered message that conforms to prevailing human desires. All too often, the church is ignorant of, if not totally indifferent toward, the weighty issue of the glory of God.

USER-FRIENDLY CHURCHES

We see this downward trend in the church in many ways. The art of preaching, once reserved for men who were courageous couriers of God's Word and whose highest aim was to uphold God's greatness, has become in too many circles nothing more than the dispensing of a man-centered message intended to pamper a worldly congregation. Preaching that attempts to unveil the supremacy of God is rare. Seldom is His majesty presented as the deepest need of the human heart. As John Piper has observed, preachers no longer believe that people are starving for the greatness of God. Vertical, God-centered preaching has been replaced with horizontal, user-friendly rhetoric that veils His glory.

Sadly, the obscuring of God's glory doesn't stop there. Much of contemporary worship waters down His greatness. Praise leaders too quickly embrace the latest musical or lyrical trends of the day—many of them trite and superficial—instead of aligning themselves with true worship that sets forth the timeless truth of God's Word. The repetitious mantra of feelings-oriented, me-focused songs that bypass Scripture always obscures God's glory.

Most tragic, however, is the way so many of us in the church deprive God of His glory by the unholy ways we live our lives before the world. It is getting more and more difficult to tell the difference between the world and the church because of how we live our lives. We have stopped trying to be different from the world and are trying instead to blend in with the present-day system by embracing its values—and vices.

During His ministry on earth, Jesus called His followers to live lives that distinguished them from the world around them. "Let your light shine before men in such a way that they may see your good works, and glorify your Father who is in heaven," He told them (Matthew 5:16). Since we are to glorify God in our lives, as Jesus said we should, we must stand out as light in a dark and adulterous generation, not step down to dwell with it in the shadows. In short, we must be different! Unfortunately, this is all too often not the case today.

The time has come for us to recover our passion for God's glory. Only then can we truly be the light in a dark world that He has called us to be.

REVIVING A PASSION FOR GOD'S GLORY

Where do we start in reviving our passion for God's glory? How do we recover what has been lost? How can we renew our heartfelt fervor for the person of God? The answer lies in this: We must focus on the primary reason for which God has made us—and that is to glorify Him (Revelation 4:11; Romans 11:36).

The Westminster Shorter Catechism begins by asking the question, "What is the chief end of man?" The answer states, "To glorify God and enjoy Him forever." In everything we do, the glory of God is to be our chief motive, our central theme, and our highest aim (1 Corinthians 10:31). God's *own* greatest passion is for His own glory, so our passion must be for His glory as well.

So what is God's glory? And if His glory is the driving reason for all that He is and does, what does that mean to us? I want us to take a look at what the Bible means by "God's glory," starting with the glory that is His simply because of who He is.

GOD'S INTRINSIC GLORY

First and foremost, God's glory refers to the sum total of all His divine attributes. It is all that He *intrinsically* is. It includes all the divine characteristics that are innately His and all the divine perfections that are inherently His—His holiness, righteousness, wrath, truth, love, grace, goodness, sovereignty, and power. God and His glory cannot be separated, for it is who He is.

For an example of what I mean by intrinsic, look around you at the created world. All the things that you see have characteristics that tell you what they are. The sun is bright, the sky is blue, and water is wet. We do not make them that way; that is what they are. One does not make the sun bright—it *is* bright. One does not make the sky blue—it *is* blue. One does not make water wet—it *is* wet. In all of these cases, the attribute is intrinsic to the object, inseparably bound to the essential nature of the thing.

It is precisely this way with God's glory. God's glory is as essential to His being as light is to the sun, as blue is to the sky, and as wet is to water. When we speak of God's glory, we mean first of all His *intrinsic* glory. It is all that God is, the whole of all His attributes, the sum total of the greatness of His divine being.

In this sense, we cannot give God glory, for He by His own nature already *is* glorious. We cannot add to or subtract from His intrinsic glory one iota. As the God who was, is, and is to come, He is forever glorious and perfect. In this sense, the glory of God is intrinsic within Himself, unaffected by outward forces or circumstances.

The Bible tells us that God's glory represents the greatness of who He is. This includes His name (Deuteronomy 28:58), His majesty (Psalm 93:1), His power (Exodus 15:6), His works (Psalm 19:1), and His holiness (Exodus 15:11). God's glory is described as great (Psalm 138:5), enduring forever (Psalm 104:31), and rich (Ephesians 3:16). This is what we call the intrinsic glory of God.

THE WEIGHT OF GLORY

In the Old Testament, the primary Hebrew word for glory (*kabod*) meant a heavy weight, such as a rich man's possessions. The greater the weight of a man's gold and silver, the richer he was. With this wealth came clout—a powerful influence on others in the community. Thus glory came to represent the greatness of a man that commanded the respect of others.

As it relates to God, His glory is the greatness of who He is—the awesome weight of His name and the infinite wealth of His divine attributes as found in His holiness, righteousness, wrath, truth, love, grace, goodness, sovereignty, and power. Every aspect of His character is immeasurably heavy and incomparably great beyond any man's character or ability. Being infinitely perfect, God is awesome in every way, a true heavyweight in every one of His divine attributes.

IT'S WHO HE IS

Because God is God, He is the only being who possesses intrinsic glory. It is His and His alone simply by virtue of who He is. God's intrinsic glory cannot change. It cannot increase, because that would mean He was previously less than perfect. Nor can it decrease, because He is eternally glorious.

Sadly, the church today often lacks a corresponding reverence for the utter profundity of God's character and attributes. Instead, frivolity and superficiality—fueled by a picture of a user-friendly god—pervades much of Christianity. I believe this can be traced back to our failure to consider the weightiness of God's most holy character.

As we refocus our view of God, a restored vision of the weight of His character will return to our hearts, leading to maturity, stability, and purity in our relationship with Him.

THE RADIANCE OF HIS GLORY

The other Hebrew word found in the Old Testament for glory (*shekinah*) describes the visible manifestation of God's holy presence, usually as light so brilliant that it cannot be looked on or approached directly. The Bible tells us that after Moses spent time with God on Mount Sinai, this glory shone through Moses' face (Exodus 34:29–35). It was the bright, shining glory cloud that descended into the tabernacle to fill the Most Holy Place (Exodus 40:34–38). When God took it up and moved it forward, that was the signal to God's people that they were to move out and follow it (Numbers 9:15–23). The people saw this divine presence—the glory of God—in an illuminating cloud by day and a pillar of fire by night. Later the same glory cloud filled the temple in Jerusalem (1 Kings 8:10–11).

This glory is the radiant manifestation of the greatness of God's holy presence. It is the visible revelation of His awesome person, most often represented by blinding light. It is God making known to man His attributes and character through creation, history, providence, His people, His Word, and Christ.

The Greek word for glory (*doxa*) also paints a mental picture of a bright, shining light—like when the shepherds were watching their flocks by night and the glory of God appeared before them, shining as brightly as the noonday sun (Luke 2:9). Another example is when Saul of Tarsus was traveling to Damascus and a blinding light (*doxa*) shone all about him, knocking him to the ground (Acts 9:3). Thus God's glory (*doxa*) refers to the shining revelation of His greatness, the manifestation of His holy character to this world. It is the emanation of His divine attributes.

SHOW ME YOUR GLORY!

It was this aspect of God's glory—His *intrinsic* glory—that Moses had in mind when he said to the Lord, "I pray Thee, show me Thy glory!" (Exodus 33:18). By that Moses meant, "God, reveal to me the greatness of who You are" or "God, make known to me the magnitude of Your awesome supremacy."

In response God said, "I Myself will make all My goodness pass before you, and will proclaim the name of the LORD before you; and I will be gracious to whom I will be gracious, and will show compassion on whom I will show compassion" (v.19).

We learn from this answer that God's name is synonymous with His glory. His is a name representing all that He is—God's glory *is* His name, His character, and His greatness. In short, His Glory is who He is. We can make no greater request than to ask God to show us His glory.

In another passage the psalmist asks, "Who is the King of glory?" (Psalm 24:8). The answer comes, "The LORD strong and mighty, The LORD mighty in battle." In this verse the word *glory* is used interchangeably with *strength* and synonymously with *might.* From that we conclude that His glory *is* His strength and His might, in addition to all His other divine attributes.

Every page of Scripture in some way declares God's greatness. David wrote, "Tell of His glory among the nations, His wonderful deeds among all the peoples. For great is the LORD, and greatly to be praised; He also is to be feared above all gods" (1 Chronicles 16:24–25). Here God's glory is seen in the performance of His great deeds. All that God does reveals the greatness of His name. Because He alone is intrinsically glorious, He alone is truly great!

Along this same line, Jesus said to Martha upon the occasion of the death of her brother, Lazarus, "Did I not say to you, if you believe, you will see the glory of God?" (John 11:40). Before her astonished eyes, Christ raised Lazarus from the dead. In Martha's case, seeing the resurrection of Lazarus was seeing God's glory because it clearly revealed the greatness of God.

When we look at the intrinsic glory of God—a reflection of

who He is—we are left with one choice and that is to give Him the glory He is due!

ASCRIBE TO HIM GLORY

The second aspect of the glory of God is what is often called His *ascribed* glory. While His intrinsic glory is who He is and the making known of His attributes to us, ascribed glory is the glory we give to God based on the manifestation of His intrinsic glory to us.

Although we cannot add to His intrinsic glory, we can give Him—or ascribe to Him—glory that comes in the form of our praise and worship as we live in a manner worthy of our calling.

In the New Testament, the Greek word for glory (*doxa*) meant "to seem, to appear." Later it came to mean "to hold an opinion of someone," especially a good or proper opinion, such as one that expresses praise or gives honor to a great person who is considered vastly superior in worth and value. Thus glory meant to have and to express a right opinion of God.

The act of giving glory to God means to ascribe greatness to His name because of His infinite holiness and surpassing majesty. It refers to the praise and honor we give Him simply because it is due His name. In other words, it is acknowledging who God really is. This we call His ascribed glory, which is the glory we are to give Him simply because it is due Him.

So how do we give God glory? Where do we start? Giving God the glory due Him will never occur in a vacuum; it will only take place when we know the truth of the intrinsic glory of God. We are able to give God ascribed glory to the very degree that He makes His intrinsic glory known. Truth is the intrinsic glory of God made known, and the more truth we know about God, the more able we are to ascribe glory to God. To find that truth we turn first to the Bible, God's written Word.

GLORY TO GOD!

In the great heavenly worship scene in the book of Revelation, all creation gives glory to God (Revelation 4:9–11). Recording what he saw, the apostle John wrote, "The living creatures give glory and honor and thanks to Him who sits on the throne, to Him who lives forever and ever." In this scene, the twenty-four elders, representing the redeemed of all ages, fall down before the one true God, saying, "Worthy are You, our Lord and our God, to receive glory and honor and power." All heaven is portrayed as giving glory to God, worshiping Him, declaring His greatness, and giving Him honor because He alone is worthy. They give Him glory because He is glorious.

The psalmist exhorts us:

> Ascribe to the LORD, O sons of the mighty,
> Ascribe to the LORD glory and strength.
> Ascribe to the LORD the glory due to His name;
> Worship the LORD in holy array.
> PSALM 29:1–2

This calls to each of us to give endless glory to God—the highest purpose for which we were created.

The apostle Paul wrote, "Now to the King eternal, immortal, invisible, the only God, be honor and glory, forever and ever. Amen" (1 Timothy 1:17). In this magnificent doxology, the apostle invites us to praise God and give Him glory—to recognize the glory of His name and acknowledge His greatness by giving Him praise.

As God's children, it is our calling—and our wonderful privilege—to honor Him who reigns as the King over all, who alone is glorious, and who alone is worthy to receive the glory He alone deserves.

We ascribe glory to God by the way we live our lives. The more our lives conform to the image of His Son, the more glory we give to Him. In all that we say and in all that we do, we are to glorify our heavenly Father.

ALL TO GOD'S GLORY

We are to give God glory with our lips, and we are to glorify Him in our actions. Living our lives committed to pleasing Him in every respect glorifies God. The apostle Paul wrote, "Whether, then, you eat or drink or whatever you do, do all to the glory of God" (1 Corinthians 10:31). Everything we do in life, even in carrying out the most basic everyday necessities such as eating and drinking, is to be done to honor Him.

We glorify God by living in a manner consistent with who He is. That is to say, we must put His character on display in our lives. His holiness must become our holiness, His love our love, and His truth our truth. This imitation glorifies Him!

The apostle Peter tells us:

> Whoever speaks, is to do as one who is speaking
> the utterances of God; whoever serves is to do so
> as one who is serving by the strength which God supplies;
> so that in all things God may be glorified through Jesus Christ,
> to whom belongs the glory and dominion forever and ever. Amen.
>
> 1 PETER 4:11

This means that glorifying God is to be the consuming purpose that dictates and dominates the whole of who we are.

The Word tells us that we are to glorify God before men so they may see a reflection of Him in us. The apostle Peter writes, "Keep your behavior excellent among the Gentiles, so that in the thing in which they slander you as evildoers, they may on account of your good deeds, as they observe them, glorify God in the day of visitation" (1 Peter 2:12).

USER-FRIENDLY WORSHIP?

In this chapter we have concentrated on the truths concerning God's glory—the glory that is His simply because He is God as well as the glory we are to give Him in word and deed. We are to glorify God in *everything* we do, which is the greatest form of praise and worship we can offer Him.

Our view of God has everything to do with how, or whether, we glorify Him with our lives. A diminished view of God demeans the worship we give to Him. The higher our view of God is, the greater our adoration for Him will be. Conversely, the lower our view of God is, the lower our worship of Him will be. Our worship will rise no higher than our thoughts of Him. We are to worship Him in spirit and truth, most specifically the truth of who He is (John 4:23–24).

Therefore, user-friendly worship is a contradiction in terms. Because it demeans the glory of the true God, it diminishes the glory given His name. At the same time, it produces shallow lives that do not reflect His true greatness and so rob Him of the glory that is rightfully His.

Inevitably, we become like who, or what, we worship. The user-friendly god can produce only a user-friendly life that fails to become all that God intends. Those with a low view of God will live, consciously or subconsciously, at a low level; and the result will be hollow lives and empty existence. Theirs will never be a life full of the joy and effectiveness that glorifies God at every turn.

There is no more joyful, contented, and godly life than one that is committed to glorifying God—the real God—who has revealed to us His intrinsic glory through the written Word.

May we be people who, in intently gazing on the unveiled glory of God, are transformed into the same image—as the Word says, "from glory to glory" (2 Corinthians 3:18). God's glory is manifested in us as we behold the greatness of His holy character and attributes. May our hearts' cry be the prayer of Moses.

Show me Your glory!

chapter eleven

THE GREATEST GLORY

The Cross of God

—

The achievement of Christ's cross
must be seen in terms of revelation
as well as salvation.

JOHN STOTT

A few years ago, I drove to Chicago with my family to speak at a men's conference. I will never forget the impression left upon us when we first saw the city's magnificent skyline. From as far away as Indiana, we could see the outline of the massive buildings of Chicago peering over the horizon.

The closer we came, the more the skyscrapers seemed to rise in height. For thirty minutes, as we headed toward the heart of this impressive city, the imposing edifices ahead of us appeared to grow out of the ground before our very eyes.

The famous Sears Tower dwarfed even the tallest of the other superstructures. As we entered downtown Chicago, this massive construction loomed even larger. Standing at its base, we gazed straight up at the 110-story building that soars more than fourteen hundred feet in the air. Built with 76,400 tons of steel, containing more than 4.5 million square feet, and covered by 16,000 bronze-tinted windows, the Sears Tower is an amazing sight to behold. We were astonished at its greatness and grandeur. The closer we drew, the larger it grew. And the larger it grew, the more we seemed to shrink.

That is what drawing close to something awesome will do. It will make you feel smaller and smaller by comparison. This is precisely the dynamic that occurs in our hearts when we draw near to the starkest, most awesome display of God's glory: the cross of Jesus Christ.

STANDING AT THE FOOT OF THE CROSS

The closer we draw to the cross of Jesus Christ, where the Son of God gave His life in order to restore our fellowship with the holy God, the higher our view of God grows. And the higher our view of Him, the smaller our view of ourselves becomes.

Towering over mankind, the Cross is the most comprehensive revelation of God's glory. At the cross, Christ, "the radiance of His glory and the exact representation of His nature" (Hebrews 1:3), poured forth the very essence of the glory that belongs to God alone. To look upon God's Son willingly dying in our place is to gaze at the fullest disclosure of God's divine attributes. We see the unveiled glory of God fully revealed in Jesus Christ's crucifixion.

DEGREES OF GLORY

Like the sun shining with varying degrees of radiance at different hours of the day, God's glory shone through His Son with varying degrees of brilliance during different times of His earthly life and ministry. Certainly the miracles Jesus performed revealed God's glory to the disciples (John 2:11). Likewise the truth He taught, the love He showed, and the way He lived all revealed God's glory to man.

During His earthly ministry, Jesus was always aware of His purpose, which was to glorify His Father. Jesus spoke of this, saying, "He who speaks from himself seeks his own glory; but He who is seeking the glory of the one who sent Him, He is true, and there is no unrighteousness in Him" (John 7:18). Jesus would magnify God's glory by doing the Father's will at the cross. As the time of His death drew near, He was in deep anguish. "Now My soul has become troubled; and what shall I say, 'Father, save Me from this hour'? But for this purpose I came to this hour. 'Father, glorify Thy name'" (John 12:27–28). Christ's highest priority was to glorify God the Father, and this He did supremely as He laid down His life for us.

Calvary was the moment when God's glory shown brightest through His one and only Son.

THE SPLENDID THEATER

The noted theologian and reformer John Calvin once wrote, "For in the cross of Christ, as in a splendid theatre, the incomparable goodness of God is set before the whole world. The glory of God shines, indeed, in all creatures on high and below, but never more brightly than in the Cross." Hidden from the eyes of an unbelieving world, Calvin wrote, the Cross is a boundless glory to us who believe: "If it be objected that nothing could be less glorious than Christ's death...I reply that in the death we see a boundless glory which is concealed from the ungodly."

Calvin was correct. Christ's death was the stage upon which God's glory was most fully unveiled. His character was made known through the unfolding drama of redemption, and at the center of the stage was Christ's victorious death for sinners.

UPPERMOST IN CHRIST'S MIND

Even in the upper room, the unveiling of this divine glory was supreme in Christ's mind. On the eve of the crucifixion, Jesus spoke of His death in these words: "Now is the Son of Man glorified, and God is glorified in Him; if God is glorified in Him, God will also glorify Him in Himself" (John 13:31–32). God's glory was uniquely displayed in Christ as He laid down His life for us.

With His mission to glorify God uppermost in His heart, Jesus led His disciples out of the upper room to the Garden of Gethsemane. His death imminent, Jesus isolated Himself for a brief time of prayer. Reaffirming His commitment to glorify the Father in His approaching death, He prayed, "Father, the hour has come; Glorify Thy Son, that the Son may glorify Thee" (John 17:1).

In Christ's humble act of laying down His life, the Father would be supremely glorified in the Son, for countless numbers down through the centuries would believe on His name and be saved.

From a human perspective, the Cross was gory; but from a divine perspective, it was glory. From man's perspective, the death of Christ was a dastardly deed, committed by rebellious men, and involved unspeakable suffering, pain, and humiliation. From God's perspective, however, it was a divine work He intentionally carried out as the supreme revelation of His own glory.

The Cross was the ultimate display of the greatness of God.

THE CROSS: GOD'S GREATNESS DISPLAYED

We should ask ourselves, *How* is God glorified in Christ's death? *How* is God's glory revealed on the cross? *How* is glory ascribed to the Father in the death of His Son?

As sunlight shining through a prism displays most brilliantly the various colors of the spectrum, so the glory of God shines fullest when it radiates through the lens of the Cross. Each divine attribute is most splendidly beheld in the incredible death of our Lord. If you want to see what God is like, look at the Cross.

Let us now look at each of God's perfect attributes as it is magnified through the perfect prism of Calvary.

SEPARATED FROM SINNERS

First, the Cross manifests the glory of *God's holiness*. In Christ's death, we clearly see that God is so pure that He cannot have fellowship with fallen man. The Bible says that God's "eyes are too pure to approve evil" (Habakkuk 1:13). God is too holy to associate with His sinful creatures. Because He is perfectly holy, He is separated from us by sin. Sinners cannot approach Him because He dwells in a remote light no man has seen or can see (1 Timothy 6:16).

The Cross underscores the fact that there is an infinite chasm separating a holy God from sinful man, an expanse that can never be bridged by man's own efforts at righteousness. Christ's death was necessary, since, as sinners, we cannot come to God while still abiding in our sin. Had there been another way for God to accept sinners apart from the Cross, God would have spared His own beloved Son. But there was no other way.

The apostle Paul wrote, "For there is one God, and one mediator also between God and men, the man Christ Jesus, who gave Himself as a ransom for all, the testimony given at the proper time" (1 Timothy 2:5–6). A mediator is one who brings two sides together when they have had a conflict and are at an impasse. According to this passage, the only way sinful man can approach a holy God is through the mediation of the Cross. Apart from it, there is no approaching God.

SIN UNDER JUDGMENT

Second, the Cross demonstrates the glory of *God's wrath*. In Jesus' substitutionary death, we see God, the moral judge of the universe, judging man's sin. At Calvary, God unleashed His righteous anger upon Christ, His own Son, who bore our sins in His body. The apostle John said, "He Himself is the propitiation for our sins" (1 John 2:2). The word *propitiation* means appeasement or satisfaction. The substitutionary death of Christ on the cross perfectly appeased the righteous demands of God's holiness as Jesus bore God's wrath for our sins.

Only those already facing God's eternal wrath in hell can begin to comprehend the divine vengeance poured out on Christ at the cross. As physically painful as death by crucifixion was, far more excruciating to Christ were His spiritual sufferings, particularly the separation from His Father. While many thousands suffered death by crucifixion in the first century, only one bore God's eternal wrath for sins.

That Christ was destined to die for the sins of the world was lost even on the disciples, who were continually with Him during His earthly ministry. When James and John approached Jesus about sitting on His right and left in His glory, He replied, "Are you able to drink the cup that I drink, or to be baptized with the baptism with which I am baptized?" (Mark 10:38). The cup to which Jesus referred was the symbol of God's wrath against our sin, which was to be poured out for Him to drink. When Jesus died for our sins, the fullness of divine fury fell on Him as He drank the extreme bitterness of the cup of wrath.

GOD'S LOVE REACHING OUT

Third, the Cross displays the glory of *God's love*. In the death of Christ, God demonstrated His love to lost sinners as He reached out to span the infinite chasm separating Him from mankind. At Calvary, the great sacrifice was made so that we might come to God. Never has unconditional love been so vividly shown than when God gave the greatest gift of all—His Son—for unworthy rebels like us.

The apostle Paul said, "But God demonstrates His own love toward us, in that while we were yet sinners, Christ died for us" (Romans 5:8).

The apostle John wrote:

> By this the love of God was manifested in us,
> that God has sent His only begotten Son
> into the world so that we might
> live through Him. In this is love,
> not that we loved God,
> but that He loved us and sent His Son
> to be the propitiation for our sins.
>
> 1 JOHN 4:9–10

The supreme evidence and expression of God's love is seen in the voluntary laying down of Christ's life for us. Jesus said, "Greater love has no one than this, that one lay down his life for his friends" (John 15:13).

GOD'S UNCHANGING PLAN

Fourth, the Cross reveals the glory of *God's unchangeableness*. At Calvary, we clearly see the immutability of God as His eternal plan of redemption was brought to fulfillment in Christ. God remained unchanged throughout successive generations of Old Testament times. Then, in the fullness of time, He sent His Son into this world to become a curse for us on the tree (Galatians 4:4).

Drafted in eternity past, God's plan of salvation was fulfilled within time. The apostle John understood this truth when He said the Lamb of God was slain in the mind of God before the foundation of the world (Revelation 13:8). Like incontrovertible facts presented in a courtroom, the Cross stands forever as the most unshakable evidence that God *never* changes.

GOD PAID THE PRICE

Fifth, the Cross reveals the glory of *God's grace.* In Christ's sacrifice for sins, we see God paying our sin debt in full so that He can offer salvation to us as a free gift. If we could earn our salvation, or even contribute to it, Christ died needlessly. But in the Cross we see the freeness of God's grace portrayed in most vivid terms.

As Jesus died bearing our sins, He cried out, "It is finished!" (John 19:30). This victorious pronouncement meant "paid in full," signifying that the work of redemption had been completed. Jesus announced that He, by His sacrifice, had paid the price for our sins and now graciously offered forgiveness and salvation as a free gift. Jesus freely provides salvation "as a gift by His grace" (Romans 3:24), a righteousness received apart from any human merit or good works on our part.

POWER OVER SIN

Sixth, the Cross reveals the glory of *God's power.* In the death and resurrection of Christ, God triumphantly defeated sin and destroyed the works of the devil. Scripture says: "The Son of God appeared for this purpose, to destroy the works of the devil" (1 John 3:8). Jesus accomplished a mighty victory on the cross.

The apostle Paul understood that there has never been a greater display of God's power than in the gospel of the Cross. He wrote, "When He had disarmed the rulers and authorities, He made a public display of them, having triumphed over them through Him" (Colossians 2:15). The apostle also boasted, "For I am not ashamed of the gospel, for it is the power of God for salvation to everyone who believes" (Romans 1:16).

The Greek word for *power (dunamis)* has evolved into the English word *dynamite,* which implies that the power of God has the ability to explode in the sinner's heart and give him new life. Greater than God's power in creation is His power unleashed in the re-creation of those who were once lost sinners. The Bible says that the message of the Cross will sound foolish to some, but it is the power of God to us who believe (1 Corinthians 1:18).

A PROMISE IS A PROMISE

Seventh, the Cross reveals the glory of *God's faithfulness.* From the days of Adam and Eve in the Garden of Eden, God had promised that a Savior would come. At the dawn of human history, four thousand years before Christ's coming, God foretold that One would come to crush the head of Satan and thereby undo the curse of sin (Genesis 3:15). He promised that the Savior would be born of the seed of Abraham (Genesis 17:7), Isaac (Genesis 21:12), Jesse (Isaiah 11:2), and David (Psalm 132:11).

Writing seven hundred years before Christ's coming, the prophet Isaiah predicted that the Messiah would:

- be born of a virgin (7:14);
- be anointed with the Spirit (11:2; 61:1);
- begin His ministry in Galilee (9:1–2);
- preach the gospel (61:1–2);

- be meek (42:2);
- be compassionate (40:11);
- suffer vicariously for others (53:4, 6, 12);
- patiently endure (53:7);
- be marred beyond recognition (52:14; 53:3);
- be spit on and scourged (50:6);
- be numbered with transgressors (53:12);
- intercede for His murderers (53:12);
- die for our sins (53:4–6, 12).

God faithfully fulfilled all of these prophecies and many more, just as He foretold, never deviating from His announced plan of redemption. Nowhere is God's faithfulness to His promises more clearly seen than in the Cross. Just as it had been written, so it came to pass.

MERCY ABOUNDING

Eighth, the Cross reveals the glory of *God's mercy.* In Christ's death we see "God, who is rich in mercy" (Ephesians 2:4, NKJV) displaying His boundless mercy toward those who actually deserve His judgment. By compassionately identifying Himself with us in our sinful state, God demonstrated that He is touched by our lost condition and feels the pain of our ruin.

The psalmist wrote:

> The LORD is merciful and gracious,
> Slow to anger, and abounding in mercy.
> He will not always strive with us,
> Nor will He keep His anger forever.
> He has not dealt with us according to our sins,

> Nor punished us according to our iniquities.
> For as the heavens are high above the earth,
> So great is His mercy toward those who fear Him.
>
> PSALM 103:8–11

What a picture of the mercy of God!

THE SHEER GENIUS OF GOD

Ninth, the Cross reveals the glory of *God's wisdom*. In the death of Christ, God displayed His own sheer genius in masterminding a plan of salvation whereby He remained both just and the justifier. If we had a million lifetimes to think and create a means by which a holy God would accept sinful man, we could never come up with the Cross. Only the inscrutable wisdom of God could have thought of it.

The apostle Paul wrote:

> For since in the wisdom of God the world
> through its wisdom did not come to know God,
> God was well-pleased through
> the foolishness of the message
> preached to save those who believe.
> For indeed Jews ask for signs,
> and Greeks search for wisdom;
> but we preach Christ crucified.
>
> 1 CORINTHIANS 1:21–22

God designed His plan of salvation in such a way that sinful man could not come to know Him by human wisdom, which would only exalt man. So God purposed to save lost sinners through a means that seemed utter nonsense to a "wise" world—the Cross.

In the Cross, we see the wisdom of God most fully revealed.

In His infinite wisdom, God designed a plan that in no way compromised His holiness or left His righteousness unfulfilled. God's wrath has been poured out on man's sin; all the while, His righteous demands have been met, and He is now free to receive sinners into His holy presence.

FROM ETERNITY TO ETERNITY

Tenth, the Cross reveals the glory of *God's eternality.* In Christ's death, the unchangeable plan of God's redemption reached back to eternity past and stretched forward to eternity future. In eternity past, three members of the Godhead counseled together and designed "so great a salvation" (Hebrews 2:3). Purposed by our triune God before time began, the Cross became the supreme outworking of God's eternal decree in time (Ephesians 1:11).

Expanding on this grand truth, the apostle Paul wrote, "He [God] chose us in Him before the foundation of the world" (Ephesians 1:4), indicating that in eternity past God chose His own unto salvation based on the death of Christ, which would make all who would believe worthy. Paul wrote that God has "saved us, and called us with a holy calling, not according to our works, but according to His own purpose and grace which was granted us in Christ Jesus from all eternity" (2 Timothy 1:9). It was according to God's eternal plan that Jesus came and made the necessary sacrifice for our sins in order to secure our salvation.

Furthermore, God's eternalness is seen by His gift offered to us in the Cross—the free gift of *eternal* life. As its very name suggests, the Cross provides that which has eternal value. Eternal life is a quality of life in which the God of eternity comes to dwell within us through our faith in Christ. The apostle recorded these words of Christ: "Truly, truly, I say to you, he who hears My word, and believes Him who sent Me, has eternal life, and does not come into judgment, but has passed out of death into life" (John 5:24).

The Cross means we will live with God—forever! Jesus said, "I am the resurrection and the life; he who believes in Me shall live even if he dies, and everyone who lives and believes in Me shall never die" (John 11:25–26). All who believe in Christ will live with God forever, praising the Lord Jesus as God's Lamb who purchased our salvation.

In heaven, the apostle John saw "a Lamb standing, as if slain" (Revelation 5:6), occupying the center place of worship, adored by saints and angels alike. What a glorious picture of eternity!

SOVEREIGN GRACE

Eleventh, the Cross reveals the glory of *God's sovereignty*. Nowhere do we see more clearly the irresistible, sovereign purposes of God being carried out than at the Cross. At Calvary, as His Son was dying, God did not passively look down the tunnel of time and observe Jesus being crucified and then, as if Jesus were merely a victim of circumstance, adopt that tragedy as His plan. On the contrary, God had planned the death of His Son, the Lamb of God, long before time began.

On the day of Pentecost, Peter declared that Jesus was put to death according to the "predetermined plan and foreknowledge of God" (Acts 2:23). Although the Roman soldiers of their own volition drove the nails into Jesus' hands and hoisted Him up on the cross, they were in reality instruments God used to carry out His foreordained plan. Although the Jewish leaders incited the mob that called for Jesus' death—and will be held accountable by God in the final judgment for their sin—they were, nevertheless, the agents God used to execute His inscrutable plan, designed before time began.

At the cross we can clearly see the overruling providence of God, as well as His sovereign grace, overriding the actions of sinful men.

A MISSING NOTE

Perhaps the greatest fallacy of the user-friendly god is how it demeans the cross of Jesus Christ. Even inadvertently, those who serve the user-friendly god may acknowledge the Cross, but they ignore the rich fullness of Christ's death, choosing instead to focus upon a man-centered message that bypasses Calvary. Any mention of the Cross that stresses sentimental, syrupy love but excludes God's holiness, wrath, and sovereignty is an incomplete picture of what God has really done through Christ on the cross.

In avoiding what Paul calls "the stumbling block of the cross" (Galatians 5:11), too many people have diluted the grace of God and done the very thing they sought to avoid—stumble at the rock of offense!

We must restore the centrality of the Cross in all its rich fullness. The crucifixion is the supreme revelation of God's glory. In the death of Christ, we see most clearly the greatness of who God is. In anchoring ourselves to the Cross, we will come to understand the excellencies of the divine attributes and savor the beauties of His holiness. Let us say, with the apostle Paul, "May it never be that I should boast, except in the cross of our Lord Jesus Christ" (Galatians 6:14).

Do you want to see a complete picture of the glory of the one true God? You need look no further than the Cross.

part three

THE EXPERIENCE

OF GOD

chapter twelve

UP CLOSE AND PERSONAL

The True Knowledge of God

—

Nothing will so enlarge the intellect,
nothing so magnify the whole soul of man,
as a devout, earnest, continued investigation
of the great subject of the Deity.
CHARLES H. SPURGEON

Anthony Collins, a famous agnostic of years past, wrote a well-known but destructive book titled *Discourse on Freethinking*. Filled with humanistic philosophy and disseminating high thoughts of man and notoriously low thoughts of God, Collins's treatise greatly impacted his day.

One Sunday, Collins encountered a poor English workingman who was walking to church. Collins thought he would belittle him, so he asked, "Where are you going?"

"To church, sir," answered the common laborer. "I am going to worship God."

Attempting to confuse the simple fellow, Collins asked him sarcastically, "Is your God a *great* God, or a *little* God?" The humble churchgoer never missed a beat. He immediately replied with an answer far more profound than what the philosopher was prepared to hear.

"My God is so great, sir," the man said, "that the heaven of heavens cannot contain Him, and so little that He can dwell within my lowly heart."

Collins was completely disarmed at such a grand thought and had no rebuttal for such a wise reply. Years later, the lettered philosopher admitted that this uneducated man had had a far more powerful effect on his sophisticated mind than all the volumes he had read that argued in favor of Christianity.

What a glorious truth! The heaven of heavens cannot contain God, yet He chooses to dwell in lowly hearts like ours when we humble ourselves before Him in repentance and faith. He is great enough to fill the heavens, yet He chooses to live within our hearts in a personal relationship with us.

This is the truth around which the whole Christian faith is built.

A DEEP, ABIDING RELATIONSHIP

The amazing truth of the Christian life is this: The awesome God who dwells on high also dwells in our lowly, humble hearts. It is a great privilege that we can intimately know this majestic, transcendent God in an intimate relationship. What a tremendous truth this is! The God of all time has chosen to reveal Himself to us personally to establish a deep, personal, abiding relationship with us.

Making this very point, God says through the prophet Isaiah:

> For thus says the high and exalted One
> Who lives forever, whose name is Holy,
> "I dwell on a high and holy place,

> And also with the contrite and lowly of spirit
> In order to revive the spirit of the lowly
> And to revive the heart of the contrite."
>
> ISAIAH 57:15

In an apparent paradox, the exalted God, who is high and lifted up and sits on a high throne in heaven, indwells lowly and humble hearts on the earth.

Isaiah went on to write:

> Thus says the LORD,
> "Heaven is My throne,
> and the earth is My footstool.
> Where then is a house you could build for Me?
> And where is a place that I may rest?
> For My hand made all these things,
> Thus all these things came into being," declares the LORD.
> "But to this one I will look,
> To him who is humble and contrite of spirit,
> and who trembles at My word.
>
> ISAIAH 66:1–2

This is a profound truth. Those who are humble, contrite of spirit, and who tremble at God's Word can know Him.

But what does it mean to actually *know* God? Not just know *about* Him, but know Him in a personal way? Why is this knowledge so important? What are the benefits to one's life, both now and forever, of truly knowing God? Why is a genuine knowledge of the true God at the heart of real Christianity? In this chapter I will address these questions.

THE TRUE KNOWLEDGE OF GOD

At its core, the knowledge of God involves entering into a personal relationship with Him. Christianity is a relationship, while religion is nothing more than man's inadequate efforts to know God through human understanding and by struggling to reach up to Him through good works. Yet in all man's striving, he cannot come to truly know this God on his own. A religionist may process some facts about God, but he cannot experientially know Him. Only personal faith in Jesus Christ leads to the true knowledge of God. In fact, the Bible says that eternal life is knowing God through Jesus Christ. Jesus said, "This is eternal life, that they may known You, the only true God, and Jesus Christ whom You have sent" (John 17:3).

Perhaps no passage communicates more clearly what a privilege it is to know God personally than Jeremiah 9:23–24. Pinpointing the singular importance of this relationship, Jeremiah recorded what God says about it:

> Thus says the LORD, "Let not a wise man
> boast of his wisdom, and let not the
> mighty man boast of his might,
> let not a rich man boast of his riches;
> but let him who boasts boast of this,
> that he understands and knows Me,
> that I am the LORD who exercises lovingkindness,
> justice, and righteousness on earth;
> for I delight in these things," declares the LORD.
>
> JEREMIAH 9:23–24

Jeremiah indicates that there is nothing greater than knowing God personally and that it is a relationship about which to boast.

In these two verses, Jeremiah charted for us several dynamic aspects of knowing God personally.

Here are some of the truths Jeremiah recorded for us concerning our personal relationship with almighty God.

The Highest Privilege

First, the knowledge of God is a *privileged relationship*. As God's mouthpiece, Jeremiah began by declaring, "Thus says the LORD." Please notice who is saying this. The speaker is none other than the LORD, the sovereign ruler over all. Unmistakably, the One who invites us into a relationship with Himself is the highest authority in the entire universe—the King of kings and Lord of lords. As we have seen, the God with whom we can enjoy fellowship is the One who has revealed Himself to us as holy, sovereign, wrathful, loving, and good.

The greater the person, the greater the privilege it is to know that individual. The more important that people are perceived to be, the more special it is to know them. For example, before I met my wife she worked for the governor of South Carolina. Anne's responsibilities as director of the governor's mansion inclued overseeing official dinners and entertaining special guests of the state. She hosted many dignitaries and notable officials, including Ronald Reagan, Gerald Ford, Bob Hope, and England's Prince Charles. We still have pictures of Anne with each of these famous people.

What makes each of these pictures so special is the status of these men. Because of their importance in the world, we attach a special significance to my wife's having known them. Their renown elevated the privilege of establishing a relationship with them, even if it was only for a short period of time.

No Greater Privilege

It is special to know important people of this world, but because of the unrivaled importance of who God is, there is no greater privilege than knowing Him. What an infinitely greater privilege it is to know the One before whom Presidents Ford and Reagan will one day bow, the One whom Prince Charles will one day confess as Lord.

Sadly, though, having a low view of God—the user-friendly god—minimizes the importance of knowing the true God. If God is not all that the Bible tells us He is—if He is more like you and me—then knowing Him is not quite so special. But if God is truly holy and sovereign, then knowing Him is everything.

Our picture of God directly affects the importance we assign to knowing Him. The greater we understand God to be, the greater we will esteem the privilege of having a personal relationship with Him.

Intimacy with God

Second, the knowledge of God is a *personal relationship*. The most striking aspect of knowing God is that it is a relationship of closest intimacy with Him. Far exceeding us in every way, God is wonderfully near all who believe upon Christ.

In Jeremiah 9:23–24, the prophet used the Hebrew word *yadah* for "know." The same word was used to describe the special relationship that exists between God and His chosen people, Israel (Amos 3:2). It also describes a close relationship with another person, like the intimacy enjoyed between a husband and wife in the marriage relationship (Genesis 4:1).

I can illustrate the meaning of this word in this way. In the course of my life, I have been privileged to know many women. My mother, grandmother, aunts, various schoolteachers, and the mothers of friends have all been close to me. I have profited greatly from my relationship with each of them. But there is only *one* woman I have known intimately in the fullest meaning of the word—spiritually, emotionally, and physically. Biblically speaking, she is the only woman I have known personally, or with whom I have become one as we have shared the depths of our lives.

In like fashion, this word *know* defines the deep, intimate, love relationship between believers and God. Marked by bonded unity, close intimacy, and transparency of the soul, this relationship could not be any more intimate. As a husband intimately knows his wife, so we can know God. By entering into a personal relationship with Him, we become one with Him, He in us and us in Him. To know God is to become intimate with Him, loving Him in the closest relationship possible.

NOTHING IS MORE IMPORTANT

Third, the knowledge of God is a *priority relationship*. Because God is holy, knowing Him should be our single most important pursuit in life. Overshadowing all other endeavors, knowing Him should be our highest priority. All earthly endeavors and human relationships are to take a back seat to this one supreme pursuit.

In Jeremiah 9:23–24, God states, "Let not a wise man boast in his wisdom"; rather, let him "boast that He knows Me." According to the prophet, a personal relationship with God is more important than any learning, education, or training anyone can receive. Worldly knowledge, whether gained through formal education or personal experience, is infinitely inferior to the true knowledge of the living God. No matter how intelligent or gifted a man is, no matter how many academic degrees he may have, no matter what amount of knowledge he possesses, it cannot compare with personally knowing God. Apart from the personal knowledge of God, all human learning and education is but vanity.

While God's Word tells us that knowing the true God is to be the most important part of our lives, we cannot experience a deep relationship with the user-friendly god. After all, having a personal relationship with one who is only moderately holy, partially sovereign, modestly wrathful, or minimally loving becomes *less* of a priority. If God alone is great, then nothing is more important than knowing Him.

PLUGGING INTO THE POWER

Fourth, the knowledge of God is a *powerful relationship*. Jeremiah went on to say, "Let not the mighty man boast of his might." Instead "Let him who boasts boast of this, that he understands and knows Me" (Jeremiah 9:23–24). This means that the spiritual power that God provides to weak people who know Him is far greater than the earthly power that people ignorant of Him gain through their own strength. No man should put his confidence in his own might, whether it is physical strength, political clout, or social influence. More important than gaining this kind of power is the spiritual power gained from knowing God.

Triumphant living comes only through knowing God. The apostle Paul wrote that he counted all things as loss "that I may know Him and the power of His resurrection and the fellowship of His sufferings" (Philippians 3:10). Knowing God is always coupled with the power of Christ's resurrection. Whatever we can achieve through our own strength is nothing compared to what we can do with God's Spirit empowering our lives. Such divine energy is unleashed in our lives as we grow in the personal knowledge of God. The greater our vision of God, the greater our power from Him.

The Bible says, "The people who know their God will display strength and take action" (Daniel 11:32). What a staggering claim!

Only people who know that their God is great will have great power to do great things for God. The knowledge of God unleashes His abundant power in their lives, energizing them in every arena of life. Regardless of the seeming impossibility of the challenge, those who know God will have great power to do His will. Those who know the greatness of God are *compelled* to do something great for God.

TREASURE OF ALL TREASURES

Fifth, the knowledge of God is a *profitable relationship*. There is no greater treasure than our relationship with the living God. "Let not a rich man boast of his riches," Jeremiah continues, but instead, "Let him boast that he knows Me" (vv. 23–24). No amount of worldly riches can compare with the spiritual riches of knowing the living God of heaven and earth.

Perhaps no greater lie exists than the one that says wealth can buy happiness. It has been said that money can buy a bed, but not sleep; acquire books, but not wisdom; purchase a house, but not a home; obtain medicine, but not health; gain entertainment, but not contentment; secure a piece of the rock, but not peace of mind. Far greater than possessing the riches of this world is knowing the God who owns it all.

Through a growing, deepening relationship with Him, we may possess true riches—*spiritual* riches. With the knowledge of God comes the incomparable wealth of His grace, which is lavished upon us in Christ Jesus. His grace brings with it the forgiveness of sins, eternal life, the Holy Spirit within us, adoption into His family, a right standing before Him, and more. All this because we have come to know God. Now this is truly a profitable relationship!

Furthermore, those who know God find great contentment in Him. The apostle Paul learned the secret of abounding while having the things of this world, as well as living contentedly without earthly possessions (Philippians 4:10–12). The heart's satisfaction lies in knowing God, regardless of what one has or does not have. No price tag can be put on the peace that comes only from knowing Him.

NOW AND FOREVERMORE

Sixth, the knowledge of God is a *permanent relationship*. When we enter into a relationship with God, it is the beginning of an eternal relationship. God says, "I am the LORD who exercises loving-kindness" (Jeremiah 9:24). The Hebrew word for "lovingkindness" (*hesed*) means God's unconditional, covenant love exercised toward His people, a steadfast commitment that is irrevocable. It denotes a permanent relationship that can never be broken, regardless of our faithfulness or unfaithfulness. The true knowledge of God ushers us into a relationship with Him that can never be severed. Even when we are faithless, He remains faithful toward us (2 Timothy 2:13).

Knowing the deep reality of this truth, the apostle Paul stated:

> For I am convinced that neither death,
> nor life, nor angels, nor principalities,
> nor things present, nor things to come,
> nor powers, nor height, nor depth,
> nor any other created thing,
> shall be able to separate us from the love of God,
> which is in Christ Jesus our Lord.
>
> ROMANS 8:38–39

God promises that He will *never* walk away from a personal relationship with us, nor will He allow anything or anyone to sever our relationship with Him.

But, sadly, many who see God as a user-friendly god believe that one can fall away from a personal relationship with Him or that God might terminate a relationship with them due to some sin in their lives. This reflects a god made in our image, not the true God. The God who has made us in His image will never let go of us.

Safeguarding the Saints

Seventh, the knowledge of God is a *protecting relationship*. In the conclusion of Jeremiah's great declaration, God identifies Himself as "the LORD who exercises…justice, and righteousness" (9:24). By this, He defines our special relationship as one in which He guards and protects us.

These two key words in the passage we are studying—justice and righteousness—are terms used in courtrooms to signify that the verdict of the judge will reward what is right and punish what is wrong. To us they mean that God will preside over our lives with perfect equity, always doing what is right, defending us when we are innocent, rewarding us when we are faithful. Knowing God brings great comfort and peace because He can be trusted to protect us when we are wronged and safeguard our souls for all eternity.

Do You Really Know Him?

Do you know God? I am not referring to a general, superficial acquaintance with Him in which you simply acknowledge His existence. Many people know about Him but don't actually know Him. God's Word tells us that knowing Him means entering into a relationship that is privileged, personal, prioritized, powerful, profitable, permanent, and protective. Such a close relationship—far different from mere external religion—comes through faith in Jesus Christ.

DO YOU KNOW HIM?

In one of his crusades years ago, Billy Graham told a story about a man who stood up at a university where the famed evangelist was speaking and said, "Mr. Graham, I don't believe in religion."

Billy said, "I agree with you. I don't believe in religion either."

The man said, "What? I thought you were a religious leader."

"Oh no, you have got me wrong," Dr. Graham replied. "I don't believe in religion, but I can tell you about a wonderful person called Jesus."

Dr. Graham then pointed out to the young man that Christianity is not a religion, but a relationship with the Creator of the universe through His Son, Jesus Christ.

There are lots of religions all over the world—there are different religions in India, Asia, Africa, and America. The user-friendly god's best friend is religion, which I define as man's self-attempts to do what only God Himself can do—bring us to Himself. But the user-friendly god cannot save anyone. Only the true God can do that. The one true God never called anyone to religion. Instead, He calls us into a relationship with Him.

When all is said and done, when the righteous Judge gives His verdict and passes sentence on our sins, there is only one question you will need to answer: "Do you know Me?"

It is time to ask yourself this question:

Do you know Him?

chapter thirteen

WHATEVER HAPPENED TO THE FEAR OF GOD?

The Reverence for God

—

He who fears God has
nothing else to fear.
CHARLES H. SPURGEON

The accomplished British statesman, W. E. Gladstone, served multiple terms as prime minister of England between 1868 and 1894. A man known for shaping his own times, he once said something that I think is very applicable to ours.

When he was on campus at Christ Church College in England, a student asked him about the changes in the British Empire he had witnessed during his lifetime. Gladstone's answer reflected the optimism of the day. The British Empire was at its zenith, the sun seemingly would never set on its flag, and confidence reigned.

Challenging his optimistic outlook, another student asked, "Sir, are we to understand that you have no anxieties for the future? Are there no adverse signs?"

The experienced statesman thought for a moment and then

answered carefully, "Yes, there is one thing that frightens me."

"What is that?" the student inquired.

"I fear," Gladstone stoically replied, "that the fear of God seems to be dying out in the minds of men."

THE DEATH OF FEAR

Unfortunately, it seems that Gladstone's fear is being realized in our time. There is today an appalling lack of the fear of God in the hearts of men, and I lay the blame primarily on the user-friendly god. Nothing has served more to remove the fear of God from the hearts of people—including too many believers. With every downward step our thoughts of God have taken, we have in like measure lost a holy reverence for Him.

Step into the average church these days, and you will likely see that the services are designed more to remove the fear of God than to promote it. It seems that everything today is geared to make us comfortable, but not convicted; amused, but not in awe. In our efforts to make seekers more at ease in church, we have downplayed the reverential awe we should feel in the presence of almighty God. We have so emphasized the horizontal aspect of our relationship—our intimacy and closeness with Him—that the vertical aspect—our reverence, awe, and fear toward Him—has been almost totally neglected.

Sit under many of the sermons being preached, listen to many of the choruses being sung, and read many of the books that are being written, and you will see that there is, for the most part, little of a high view of God being spoken, sung, or read about. As a result, there is very little that would instill in hearts a healthy, holy fear of God.

We live in a day in which a god made in our own image has swept into our churches like a flood, and with it has come an unhealthy casualness toward God that often borders on blasphemy.

A WORLD OF DIFFERENCE

There is quite a contrast between our approach to God today and that of the biblical saints. We read in the Bible that whenever God revealed Himself to men, they were awestruck and usually fell to the ground, as did Job (Job 42:5–6), Isaiah (Isaiah 6:5), Peter (Luke 5:8), and John (Revelation 1:17). Their reactions are a far cry from the responses to God we see on the contemporary spiritual landscape, which are often frivolous, trite, cavalier, or even silly attitudes toward His glorious person.

Where is the fear of God today? Where is that reverential awe that we should rightly have when we approach the almighty God, the Creator and Sustainer of all that exists?

I certainly do not want to suggest that there should be no inward feelings or outward expressions of genuine joy overflowing in a contagious spirit of celebration toward God (Luke 2:10; Philippians 4:4; Galatians 5:22). Nor would I suggest that we should not enjoy an intimate relationship with God. God *has,* in fact, provided us marvelous access into His presence through Christ (Romans 5:5; Hebrews 4:16; 10:19–22). He has even established a Father-child relationship with us in which He promises to be our provider, protector, and friend. God desires closeness and fellowship with us as His very own people, and He pours His joy into our hearts (John 15:11).

But as we approach God, we must remember the other aspect of our relationship with Him—that He is the thrice-holy God of heaven and earth who should rightly cause fear in the hearts of all who draw close to Him. Joy comes only to the heart that genuinely fears God. In other words, reverence is the forerunner of rejoicing.

In this era of a user-friendly god, it seems that many do not like to talk about fearing God. Loving God is the overwhelming emphasis of the day, but unfortunately, to the exclusion of reverencing

Him with godly fear. You can follow God, obey God, even express incredible admiration for God, they say. All of these things are appropriate, and none of us have a problem with them. But fearing God? That seems like something out of another era.

I think that part of the problem we have with fearing God is that we don't fully understand what the word *fear* in the Bible really means—what it is and what it is not. But we must understand it, for the fear of God is the prerequisite for a strong, growing relationship with Him.

WHAT IS THE FEAR OF GOD?

What comes to your mind when you think about fearing God? Do you have a mental picture of a person cringing in the corner, cowering before God? Or do you think of a person who never smiles or laughs? Maybe you imagine someone who dresses in black, carries a big family Bible, and speaks with a lot of thees and thous. If any of these images—or many others like them—come to your mind when you think about the fear of God, then you have an inaccurate picture of what it means to fear Him.

At the very core of saving faith, there is always a healthy, holy fear of God that causes a believer to tremble. No one giggles his way into the kingdom of God. All who enter through the narrow gate that leads to life come with godly fear, brokenness, and mourning over their sin (Matthew 5:3–4; 7:13–14). As we walk by faith on the narrow path of the Christian life, we grow in our proper reverence for God. But this fear is nothing like the kind of fright a young boy feels when he sees the neighborhood bully walking threateningly toward him. It is more like the awe and respect that the same young boy would feel were he to stand before the president of the United States in the Oval Office. Just being there would cause him to feel reverence and awe. So it is with the one who rightly trembles before the Lord.

There is a world of difference between common respect for a great man and reverential awe for a great God. The English poet Charles Lamb once said, "If Shakespeare were to come into this room, we should all rise up to meet him, but if Christ were to come into it, we should all fall down and try to kiss the hem of His garment."

Fearing God is a heart attitude of worshipful submission to Him. It is a reverential awe for God in which we recognize Him for who He is—the holy, sovereign, righteous God who loves us and desires to have fellowship with us. In coming face-to-face with His holiness, we are overwhelmed and struck with the sheer glory of His being. Fearing God means to live a God-centered life in which our entire beings revolve around Him, not ourselves. It means we take Him very seriously, not superficially.

A proper fear of God begins when we realize that our lives are in His hands and that He is free to do with us as He pleases. All our days, all our circumstances, all our successes, and all our trials are under God's control, and He is guiding our lives according to His eternal plan. Fearing God includes coming to the place where we understand that everything is "from Him and through Him and to Him" (Romans 11:36). It involves the awareness that we live on His planet, breathe His air, enjoy His provisions, and live the life He has given us to live. In brief, it means recognizing that our lives revolve around *Him,* not ourselves.

THE ABCs OF FAITH

The Bible tells us that a proper fear of God is the starting point for every aspect of our relationship with God. When Solomon wrote,

"The fear of the LORD is the beginning of knowledge" (Proverbs 1:7), he meant that the true knowledge of God always begins with a deep reverence for Him. Simply put, we are to take our God very seriously; and until we do, we won't know Him personally for who He truly is. Fearing Him is the first, controlling principle that ushers us out of the kingdom of darkness into God's kingdom of light. It is the foundation of our walk with Him.

We should never outgrow a healthy, reverential awe of God. At the end of Solomon's soul-searching pursuit of the meaning in life, he said, "The conclusion, when all has been heard, is: fear God and keep His commandments, because this applies to every person" (Ecclesiastes 12:13). In other words, fearing God is not only the beginning of wisdom but also the bottom line of our lives. Sadly, though, there are few today, even among Bible-believing Christians, who really understand how important it is to fear God.

AN ALARMING DEPARTURE

Much of what transpires in the church today, as well-meaning as it may be, downplays the fear aspect of our relationship with God and actually works against promoting the awe that is the very beginning of salvation and sanctification. Man-centered preaching, some "praise choruses," and most drama—all common in today's churches—often do little, if anything, to promote the fear of God. Instead, they stroke the flesh, pamper egos, entertain the soul, tickle our ears, and address superficial "felt needs."

Preaching, music, and drama are all outstanding tools of ministry—only if they put God in His proper place. But we miss the mark when we look at God as an equal rather than looking up to Him as the sovereign, all-powerful Creator of the universe. A man-centered message and a horizontal ministry result in spiritually immature believers at best, and self-deceived, false converts at worst.

Without the fear of God, everything eternal and lasting is thrown to the wind. If we do not properly fear God, we cannot properly understand the boundless grace, mercy, and love that He has poured out on us through the Lord Jesus Christ. To paraphrase Solomon: Understanding the fear of God is the beginning point of understanding everything else about Him.

Let's take a closer look at the book of Proverbs—the one book in the Bible that has more to say about this subject than any other book—to discover how we can reverence God more and what the hallmarks of a healthy fear of God are.

CULTIVATING A HOLY FEAR

Proverbs makes it clear that we are to approach God with fear, a reverential awe because of who He is. But how can we increase that kind of fear in our hearts? How *can* we rightly grow to fear Him more? Providing us with Spirit-led insight into this vital subject, Solomon wrote:

> My son, if you will receive my sayings,
> And treasure my commandments within you,
> Make your ear attentive to wisdom,
> Incline your heart to understanding;
> For if you cry for discernment,
> Lift your voice for understanding;
> If you seek her as silver,
> And search for her as for hidden treasures;
> Then you will discern the fear of the LORD,
> And discover the knowledge of God.
>
> PROVERBS 2:1-5

Solomon established a noticeable cause and effect in this passage. He says that *if* we will receive God's Word (vv. 1–4) *then* we will fear Him (v. 5). The depth of our intake of His Word determines the depth of our fear of God. If we will explore God's Word as a prospector explores the hills seeking gold, we will discover the fear of the Lord. Reverencing God comes from receiving His Word into our hearts. To know Him is to fear Him.

To further understand this truth, consider the apostle John, who, on Patmos, was caught up in the spirit and heard a penetrating sound like a trumpet (Revelation 1:9–20). It was the voice of the Lord Jesus Christ declaring, "Write in a book what you see, and send it to the seven churches" (v. 11). As the startled apostle turned, he saw an awesome sight:

> Seven golden lampstands, and in the midst
> of the seven lampstands
> One like the Son of Man, clothed with a
> garment down to the feet and girded
> about the chest with a golden band.
> His head and His hair were white like wool,
> as white as snow, and His eyes like a flame of fire;
> His feet were like fine brass, as if refined in a furnace,
> and His voice as the sound of many waters.
> REVELATION 1:12–15, NKJV

What a breathtaking picture of divine majesty, splendor, and might!

How did John respond to what he saw? Yawn? High-five Jesus? Snuggle up to Him? Hardly! In absolute dread, the awestruck apostle collapsed at His nail-pierced feet as though he were a dead man. Remember, this is the same John who had been with the Lord during His earthly ministry and had rested his head upon His bosom in the upper room! Yet this vision of the risen, reigning Christ caused John to fall on his face. John was seized with fear because he saw the Lord as He *really* is.

EXPERIENCING THE FEAR OF GOD

Do you want to fear God? Then you need to see Jesus as John did. You need a picture of Christ reigning as the glorified Savior. To do that, you need to get into His Word and allow His Word to get into you. If you delve into the Scriptures with an open heart, you too will have a Patmos-like experience—you will hear His voice and see Him in His glorified state. Such a vision will lead to the fear of God.

You may well be asking, "What will the evidence be of fearing God in my life? How can I know if I am a true God-fearer? What can I expect to see in my life if I grow to a deeper level of fearing God?"

As we continue to look at selected verses of Proverbs, you will see that the positive, desirable fruit of fearing God is a life of holiness, health, heritage, humility, happiness, and honor.

A LIFE OF HOLINESS

First, the fear of God will lead to a life of *holiness*. Solomon wrote:

> Fear the LORD and turn away from evil.
> PROVERBS 3:7

Fearing God means that I fear displeasing Him. There is a cause and effect relationship between fearing God and turning away from evil; the former causes the latter. If we reverence Him, we will avoid all that displeases Him.

Whenever we sin, it is simply because at that moment we desire that particular sin more than we fear God. Picture a pair of scales in your mind. On one side is our fleshly desire for evil, and on the other is our healthy fear of God. Whenever our desire for sin is greater than our fear of God, we will choose to sin, tilting the scales in the wrong direction. Conversely, whenever our fear of God outweighs our desire for a particular sin, we will refuse to choose that sin, tilting the scale in the right direction. The more we are filled with awe for God, the more we will choose to obey Him and not sin against Him.

Solomon said:

> The fear of the LORD is to hate evil.
>
> PROVERBS 8:13, ITALICS MINE

This means that fearing God will lead us to hate the sin that allures us. The fear of God and the love for sin cannot coexist in the same heart. The presence of one will always displace the other.

Do you want victory over sin? Do you want to see sin the way God sees it? Then learn to fear Him!

FEARING THE HOLY ONE

After Solomon noted that the "fear of the LORD is the beginning of wisdom," he added, "the knowledge of the Holy One is understanding" (Proverbs 9:10). This says that the fear of the LORD will lead to personal knowledge of the Holy One. As we reverence Him in our hearts, we grow in our personal knowledge of His holiness.

Because we become like whomever or whatever we worship, if we reverence a holy God, we, by necessity, will grow in personal holiness. If we fear a holy God, we will hate the sin He hates, especially the sin in our own lives. A user-friendly view of God, on the other hand, lessens our fear of God and so lessens our personal holiness. As surely as day leads to night, low views of God lead to low living. Whenever we weaken our understanding of who God is, we weaken our resolve to resist temptation and we fall into sin.

The most loving thing I can do for you is lead you to fear God. The wisest thing pastors can do for their congregations is to teach them to fear God. If parents want their children to live pure and godly lives, they must teach them to fear God!

PROLONGING YOUR LIFE

Second, the fear of God will lead to a life of *health*. Solomon wrote,

The fear of the LORD prolongs life,
But the years of the wicked will be shortened.

PROVERBS 10:27

Reverencing God will extend the longevity of our days here on the earth. Let me point out that this is not a hard and fast promise from God, but a wise observation about life that is generally true. For example, the one who fears God will not be a drunkard. It is a medical fact that alcoholics are more prone to die early from maladies such as cirrhosis of the liver. The one who fears God will remain sexually pure and be less likely to die from the effects of sexually transmitted diseases like AIDS, gonorrhea, or syphilis. Although this verse does not promise good health, it does indicate that fearing God will promote purity and, therefore, health.

Expanding on this truth, Solomon added:

The fear of the LORD is a fountain of life.

PROVERBS 14:27

The Spanish explorer Ponce de León searched the New World looking for the Fountain of Youth, but he never found it. We who fear God, however, *have* discovered it. The fear of God, Proverbs says, is a fountain of life that leads to physical, emotional, and spiritual health. Fearing God can add years to your life and life to your years.

The Bible speaks about the one who commits a sin unto death (1 John 5:16–17; 1 Corinthians 11:30). Some believers die prematurely because they have become caught up in a sin for which God will take them home early. Perhaps they have become useless to God, or an embarrassment to Him, or maybe they have committed a serious sin against Him. In such cases, their sin may lead to their untimely deaths simply because they failed to fear God.

FOR GENERATIONS TO COME

Third, the fear of God results in a life of heritage. Solomon further observed:

> In the fear of the LORD there is strong confidence,
> And his children will have refuge.
>
> PROVERBS 14:26

This means that the one who fears God will influence his or her children to do the same. The apple never falls far from the tree. Although there are exceptions to the rule, God-fearing parents usually produce God-fearing children. We can leave our children no greater legacy than the fear of God.

This has been true in my own life. I grew up in a God-fearing home under the influence of parents who took their relationship with God very seriously. Their reverence for God was contagious, and it spread to me, which led me to hold Him in highest esteem. I am grateful to find refuge in the fear of God that was passed down to me. My wife and I are passing on the fear of the Lord to our children, increasing our heritage. There is no greater joy for parents than to see their children following the Lord. This is cultivated in a home environment where there is reverance for God.

A LOWLY WALK

Fourth, the fear of God will produce a life of *humility*. Solomon continued:

> The fear of the LORD is the instruction for wisdom,
> And before honor comes humility.
> PROVERBS 15:33

This wise man noted that fearing God produces humility in us. Proud people do not fear God, but humble people do. The one who reverences God will bend the knee before Him and obey His Word.

How important is humility to the Christian life? It is indispensable, especially when you consider that the only person God will honor is a humble person. The Bible says, "God is opposed to the proud, but gives grace to the humble" (1 Peter 5:5), and "everyone who exalts himself shall be humbled, but he who humbles himself shall be exalted" (Luke 18:14; cf. 14:11).

God always sings solo—He never shares His spotlight with anyone! A. W. Tozer once said, "God will only use those with whom His glory is safe."

Do you want to be mightily used of God? Then humble yourself before the Lord. How can you be filled with genuine humility? The person who is humble is the one who fears God. Therefore, reverence the Lord, and you will be clothed with humility.

THE FEAR THAT FULFILLS

Fifth, the fear of God leads to a life of *happiness*. Solomon wrote:

> The fear of the LORD leads to life,
> So that one may sleep satisfied,
> Untouched by evil.
> PROVERBS 19:23

By this, we can conclude that the fear of God drives out all other fears that would steal our peace. Centuries ago, Augustine noted, "Thou hast made us for Thine own, O Lord, and our hearts are restless until they rest in Thee." Hearts that are devoid of God are restless; but those that rest in Him, fearing His name, are filled with peace, contentment, and happiness.

Fear leads to peace, contentment, and happiness? This is a great paradox in the Christian life. But rest assured, fear—when it is the fear of God—*does* lead to joy because reverencing His name drives from our hearts those things that steal away our happiness.

Do you want true rest, peace, happiness, and joy? Then abide in the fear of God. Do you want to dispose of fear and anxiety? Then fear God. Those who fear God can lie down at night and sleep peacefully because they trust Him with their problems. Instead of being consumed with anxiety, God-fearing people are consumed with God.

THE REWARD OF REVERENCE

Sixth, the fear of God leads to a life of *honor*. Solomon said:

> The reward of humility and the fear of the LORD
> Are riches, honor and life.
> PROVERBS 22:4

The one who fears God will honor Him, and God, in turn, will honor that person. Reverencing the Lord leads to receiving His abundant blessings. Fearing God leads to His many benefits being lavished upon us. Primarily, God's spiritual riches are in view here. This *may* include, but does not necessitate, His material blessing. Again this is a maxim of life that is generally true, but not intended to be taken as a promise.

In God's kingdom the way up is down. God honors us when we honor Him through reverential awe. "Riches, honor, and life," Solomon told us, become ours as we fear God.

Would you be spiritually rich? Fear God. Would you be honored? Fear God. Would you live life abundantly? Then fear God. A high regard for God is the highroad that leads to the fullest experience of His blessings.

REVERENCING THE HOLY ONE

We have considered these truths about fearing God because only a high view of God promotes the reverential awe rightly due His name. Only as we have the true knowledge of God, focused and fixed on the fullness of His divine attributes, will we fear Him. Only an awesome God produces awe—it is that simple.

But the user-friendly god inspires no such fear. A god made in our image is a manageable deity—a god who is safe to acknowledge and approach but who instills no trembling in the heart and commands no respect. The user-friendly god is one who needs us more than we need him. He is to be helped, not honored; assisted, not adored; pitied, not praised.

The fatal flaw of the user-friendly god is that he elicits *no* fear, which is central to the godly life. If we are to see a revival in the fear of God, we must repent of our low views of God and return to the true knowledge of the One who is high and lifted up, enthroned in the heavens, majestic in holiness, strong in wrath, and steadfast in love. Only when we restore a high view of God will we see the fear of the Lord renewed in the lives of believers everywhere.

I could not agree more with W. E. Gladstone. I am concerned now, just as he was over a century ago, that the fear of God is vanishing from our hearts—even those of us who are called by His name.

There is only one antidote for such a fatal disease. We need to inject a healthy dose of a transcendent view of God into the body of Christ. Only the true knowledge of God will cure our present-day ills and restore spiritual health to our hearts.

I call upon you, grow in the knowledge of God because only as you grow to know Him who is holy will you grow in reverence, respect, and awe.

chapter fourteen

HIGH AND LIFTED UP

The Exaltation of God

*The greatest need of the moment
is that lighthearted, superficial religionists
be struck down with a vision of God high and
lifted up, with his train filling the temple.*

A. W. TOZER

Thomas K. Beecher once filled the pulpit for his prominent brother, Henry Ward Beecher, at the Plymouth Church in Brooklyn, New York. On that particular Sunday over a century ago, many curious seekers had come to hear Henry preach.

When the lesser-known Beecher appeared in the pulpit, many in the crowd got up and headed for the doors. Sensing their disappointment that his brother would not be delivering the message, Thomas raised his hand to catch their attention. Those departing the service stopped, and Thomas said, "All those who came here this morning to worship Henry Ward Beecher may withdraw from the church, but all who came to worship God may remain."

That arresting statement jolted the people to their senses, and many who were leaving returned to their pews. Beecher's sobering challenge awakened the people to the fact that they had come to worship a man when they should have been there to worship God.

We face the same challenge today.

A HIGH VIEW OF GOD

I believe people are leaving churches in such large numbers today because we have failed to hold up before them a high view of God—a vision so awesome and transcendent that it captures their hearts and changes their lives.

Because our modern-day teaching and preaching so often present a low view of God, worshipers tend to become fixated on pastors, musicians, recording artists, and other human personalities. Instead of focusing on Him, our attention is riveted on mere men. Discontented people are leaving churches in droves. Although they often point to the failure of the church or the minister to meet their needs, the real reason is because the god presented to them falls miserably short of the God set forth in the Bible. No wonder their hearts are restless, bored, and frustrated!

If our churches are to return to being the houses of worship God wants them to be, we must renew a dominant vision of God who is high and lifted up, towering in the heavens, majestic in the beauty of His holiness. We need a vision of God who is different from us, someone who is truly worthy to be worshiped and adored. In short, we are in need of a fresh dose of the majesty of God. Only as we return to our principal calling, that of displaying the true greatness of God, will people eagerly return to Him—and to church.

Such a fresh vision of God will transform us from the inside out and empower us to fulfill His calling upon our lives. That is what is missing in this day of trendy, low-commitment, user-friendly Christianity. And until we recover the true picture of God, we will languish in spiritual impotence.

Perhaps nowhere else in Scripture do we see a more vivid picture of the lofty grandeur of God than in the sixth chapter of Isaiah. Writing more than seven hundred years before the coming of Christ, the prophet Isaiah documented for us one of the most dramatic, awe-inspiring self-disclosures of God found in all of Scripture. In this monumental chapter, there is a magnificent unveiling of God's glory. Isaiah's vision provides us with the fitting place to bring this book to an appropriate conclusion.

AN HOUR OF CRISIS

As Isaiah's vision unfolds, the prophet finds himself in an hour of crisis on both the national and personal level. He records that it occurred "in the year of King Uzziah's death" (Isaiah 6:1), or in 740 B.C. Israel had been dealt a devastating blow when King Uzziah, their monarch of fifty-two years, had died. For more than five decades the nation had prospered under his leadership. As long as Uzziah was on the throne, the people were filled with strength, security, and hope for the future.

However, the foundations of the nation were shaken when the king died suddenly and left the throne of Israel unoccupied. Uzziah was the only king most of the people had ever known. Overwhelmed with the fear of the unknown, they were gripped by insecurity. Feeling the anxiety of his people, Isaiah went into the temple to seek the Lord and there, unexpectedly, received a vision of God that changed his life. So it must change ours.

It was an unveiling of who God is, and it is a vision that must change our lives as well. Only a vision of God that reveals His unsurpassed glory is powerful enough to impact and remold our lives into what God desires us to be. Let us now see God as Isaiah saw Him—sovereign, holy, wrathful, loving, and good. Each component of this vision will review for us the essential truths about God that we have examined in this book.

THE THRONE IS STILL OCCUPIED

First, Isaiah saw a vision of *God's sovereignty.* As the prophet entered the temple, he was supernaturally enabled to see beyond his earthly surroundings into the heavenly realm. With the inner eye of faith, he was enabled to see "the LORD sitting on a throne, lofty and exalted" (Isaiah 6:1). In the absence of Israel's earthly king, Isaiah saw the heavenly King.

What Isaiah saw about God is most important. The prophet viewed Him *seated* on His throne. Despite the chaos of Israel's crumbling world and despite the fact that their throne was now empty, the heavenly throne above was *still* occupied.

God's throne is high and exalted, greatly elevated above all creation, the center of the universe, the place from which He rules and reigns over the works of His hands. This is precisely what the psalmist declared when he wrote:

> God is in the heavens;
> He does whatever He pleases
>
> PSALM 115:3

Seated upon His throne, God is presiding over every other ruler, whether human or angelic, and is governing all realms of His creation. The prophet said:

> In the year of King Uzziah's death
> I saw the LORD sitting on a throne
> lofty and exalted, with the train of
> His robe filling the temple.
>
> ISAIAH 6:1

The greatness of an ancient king was measured by the size of the train of his royal robe. When Isaiah saw the Lord's robe filling the entire temple, he perceived that God's infinite greatness can be neither measured nor contained.

It is precisely this vision of God's sovereignty that must be recovered in the church today. We must rid ourselves of our silly perception of an anemic god trying to run a universe seemingly out of his control. Enough of a "designer" deity who tries to defeat the devil, but never gains the upper hand. Enough of a pathetic god who cannot prevent bad things from happening to good people.

God is still sovereign! The throne is still occupied! The King is still in control!

Do you need to recapture a vision of God's sovereignty? Do you understand that God rules over everything in the heavens? Do you know that no purpose of God can be thwarted or stymied? Do you see that God causes all things to work together for our good? If not, it is time you got a fresh picture of the sovereign God.

This is the God we serve!

SET APART AND SINLESS

Second, Isaiah saw a vision of *God's holiness*. As the prophet continued to describe his encounter with God, he wrote:

Seraphim stood above Him,
each having six wings:
with two he covered his face,
and with two he covered his feet,
and with two he flew.

ISAIAH 6:2

Each of these exalted angels covers its face with two wings, shielding its eyes from looking upon God in His dazzling glory, acknowledging His sovereignty. With two more wings they cover their feet, showing humility and acknowledging their unworthiness to be in God's presence. With the other two wings they fly, acknowledging their eagerness to serve and obey God.

Yet what they were saying is even more extraordinary. These seraphim were chanting:

Holy, Holy, Holy, is the LORD of hosts,
The whole earth is full of His glory.

ISAIAH 6:3

This threefold repetition is intentional. It conveys the superlative degree and means "Holy, Holier, Holiest." This angelic anthem testifies that God is the absolute holiest being in the entire universe, the set apart, sinless Sovereign on His throne.

Unquestionably, we desperately need to catch this vision of God's holiness. Creating a user-friendly god is an attempt to lower our holy God to man's level in order to accommodate our own sinful ways. But God is absolutely holy, and an infinite gulf separates Him from us who are sinful creatures. We can never bridge this chasm through our own efforts.

Have you come to see a vision of God's holiness? Do you see that He, in His holiness, is unapproachable by sinful man? Do you understand that He is infinitely separated from the pollution of our sin? Do you know that He cannot fellowship with those who remain in their sin?

This is the holiness of God!

HOLY SMOKE!

Third, Isaiah saw a vision of *God's wrath*. The prophet continued:

> And the foundations of the thresholds
> trembled at the voice of him who called out,
> while the temple was filling with smoke.
>
> ISAIAH 6:4

In this scene, we see God's unchanging judgment on all sin. The shaking of heaven's foundations and spewing of smoke represent God's violent reaction to man's sin. The whole temple floor began to rock beneath Isaiah's trembling feet as though an earthquake were occurring. This riveting scene reveals God's fierce wrath and inflexible judgment against all who violate His holiness.

Having witnessed God's judgment on sin, Isaiah was personally devastated, and he confessed:

> Woe is me, for I am ruined!
> Because I am a man of unclean lips,
> And I live among a people of unclean lips;
> For my eyes have seen the King, the LORD of hosts.
>
> ISAIAH 6:5

Confronted by his own sin, Isaiah declared how deserving he was of God's judgment. When he said, "Woe is me," the prophet acknowledged that he deserved to be cursed and damned by this holy God. "I am ruined," he lamented, expressing that he was a broken man, smitten and shattered. Then he confessed that the best thing about him—his lips—were unclean, a humbling admission for a prophet.

A SOUL-SHATTERING EXPERIENCE

Isaiah was unraveling like a cheap sweater for one simple reason: "For my eyes have seen the King, the LORD of hosts," he said. Whenever one sees God's holiness, one always sees his own sin. Such was Isaiah's soul-shattering, painful experience. It must be ours as well. The theology of the user-friendly god, however, downplays this aspect of God's wrath and would have us bypass this spiritual catharsis.

There are a number of preachers today, some of them quite famous, who do not want to say anything about sinful human nature or God's wrath. They label their approach to Christianity "possibility thinking" and argue that people are already so discouraged about themselves that they do not need to be told they are wicked. But the truth is there is no possibility for men to be cleansed until they know they are wicked.

So, we must recapture a vision of God's wrath. Any picture of God that avoids His violent reaction against sin—even *our* sin—is a god of our own making, a figment of our fallen imagination. This god in no way represents the true God. Away with images of a god who is indifferent toward iniquity. Away with images of one who is apathetic about sin.

Have you seen a vision of God in which He hates sin—*all* sin?

Do you understand it is a terrifying thing to fall into the hands of the living God? Do you know Him as a wrathful God who must punish sin?

If so, you have seen a vital aspect of the character of the one true God, and you are ready to receive His forgiveness.

FULL OF FORGIVENESS

Fourth, Isaiah saw a vision of *God's love*. As his understanding of God unfolded, Isaiah discovered that God is quick to forgive based upon His divinely required sacrifice for sin. The prophet wrote:

> Then one of the seraphim flew to me,
>   with a burning coal in his hand
>   which he had taken from the altar with tongs.
>
> ISAIAH 6:6

The hot coal taken from the altar of incense represents God's purifying work in cleansing us from sin. The temple altar was the place where sacrifice for sin was made through a blood atonement. Glowing, red-hot coals were placed on the altar on the Day of Atonement when the sacrifice for sin was made for forgiveness.

This sacrificial scene foreshadows the coming of God's Lamb, the Lord Jesus Christ, who would one day lay down His life on the altar of Calvary's cross in order to take away our sins. The apostle Peter wrote of Christ, "He Himself bore our sins in His body on the cross" (1 Peter 2:24) and "Christ also died for sins once for all, the just for the unjust, so that He might bring us to God" (1 Peter 3:18).

Christ's substitutionary sacrifice, prefigured in the hot coals taken from the altar where Old Testament sacrifices were made, is the basis for God's forgiveness being extended to us. Jesus "has been manifested to put away sin by the sacrifice of Himself" (Hebrews 9:26).

Isaiah then testified:

> He touched my mouth with it and said,
> "Behold, this has touched your lips;
> and your iniquity is taken away,
> and your sin is forgiven."
>
> ISAIAH 6:7

The forgiveness secured by this sacrifice was applied to the prophet, who had confessed his sin. He was immediately, fully, and freely forgiven of his iniquity.

Such cleansing is always made available to us when we confess our sins: "If we confess our sins, He is faithful and righteous to forgive us our sins and to cleanse us from all unrighteousness" (1 John 1:9).

Contrary to what this passage teaches, the message of the user-friendly god is that he will use unclean instruments just as they are. Regardless of unconfessed, unrepented sin, this god will take what he can get. According to this view of god, sin and unholiness do not disqualify anyone from ministry. Whether or not one repents, God automatically forgives. There are no negative consequences, and no one has to go through the painful experience of dealing with that sin.

This is definitely a distortion of the true knowledge of God. He always requires our confession if the burning coal is to be pressed to our sinful lips. Only then can forgiveness be applied and made real.

GOD OF A SECOND CHANCE

Fifth, Isaiah saw a vision of God's goodness. The prophet was now cleansed, and God promptly commissioned him back into His work. Isaiah recorded:

> Then I heard the voice of the LORD,
> saying, "Whom shall I send,
> and who will go for Us?"
>
> ISAIAH 6:8

With these two questions, God graciously invited the purified prophet to step forward to serve Him.

These inquiries were designed to reenlist Isaiah in the Lord's work. Here is God's goodness on display. His mercy is clearly seen in restoring His prophet to the service to which he had already given himself. How gracious of God to offer this second opportunity for service to one who had transgressed His law. God is a God of the second chance, a God who sends us back to His work when we confess our sin.

While in the belly of a great fish, the prophet Jonah learned this lesson of God's willingness to resend servants who have failed Him (Jonah 2). The apostle Peter learned this lesson after denying the Lord before men (John 21:15–17). Isaiah also learned this lesson. We must too. God gives second chances!

In broken humility, Isaiah stepped forward, saying, "Here am I. Send me!" (Isaiah 6:8). His heart was melted by God's gracious kindness, and he responded in contrite submission, offering himself to the Lord. Making himself wholly available, Isaiah expressed his willingness to do God's will and work.

As with Isaiah, so with us today. I don't care how you have sinned or failed God; He desires to reenlist you in His service.

There may be residual consequences of your sinful choices that carry into the future, but if you confess your sin, God will fully forgive you and use you again, simply because of His unconditional love and goodness.

A VISION OF GOD'S GLORY

In this passage, we see Isaiah receiving a vision of God's glory. Each of these divine attributes—His sovereignty, holiness, wrath, love, and goodness—come together to comprise God's magnificent glory, the sum of all His divine perfection. Here is the fullness of God being made known to the prophet.

Writing about Isaiah's awesome vision of God, the apostle John said that it was the glory of God that the prophet witnessed:

> These things Isaiah said because
> he saw His glory, and spoke of Him.
>
> JOHN 12:41

When he saw God—enthroned in the heavens, en-circled by angelic worshipers, rendering judgment, and providing forgiveness—Isaiah saw the fullness of the unveiled glory of God.

In reality, what the prophet saw in this vision in the temple was the revelation of the Lord Jesus Christ Himself (John 12:37–40). He saw the glory of God unveiled before his awestruck eyes in the person of God's Son, the enthroned Christ.

NOT A "USER-FRIENDLY GOD"

Obviously, it was no user-friendly god that Isaiah had seen. To the contrary, the prophet was overwhelmed with a lofty vision of the one true God. So awesome was the picture of God revealed that the prophet was radically transformed never to be the same again. Convicted, cleansed, and commissioned, he was sent to fulfill God's plan in the midst of a dark and difficult hour.

Such a life-changing vision of God may be ours—in fact, *must* be ours—as we behold Him who is high and lifted up in the pages of Scripture. Throughout the Bible, we see what Isaiah saw—God unrivaled in sovereignty, unblemished in holiness, unrestrained in wrath, undeniable in love, and unmatchable in goodness. If God is to use us mightily, we, too, must have an encounter with Him who is high and lifted up.

The user-friendly god will *never* convict us of sin or compel us to reach our generation for Christ. A low view of God will only leave us cold, complacent, compromising, even carnal. A glorious vision of a great God, however, will energize us to do great things for Him in the supernatural power He alone provides.

Let us rise up to be a part of a new generation of Isaiahs who receive a renewed vision of God in this day. Only then will we turn this world upside down for Christ.

As we have seen throughout this book, the most important thing about us is who we believe God is. Our personal knowledge of God is the primary cause of which everything else is the effect.

A faulty view of God will inevitably lead to a faulty relationship with Him, and that in turn will lead to faulty living. But a high view of God will just as surely lead to a growing, loving relationship with Him, one that will in turn lead to holy living.

THE ULTIMATE PARADIGM

The true knowledge of God is the only paradigm through which we can properly see the world around us. How you see Him dictates how you see everything else. A proper view of God brings everything else into focus.

A right view of God is everything. Without it, you have nothing. Only when God is put in the right perspective is everything else brought into focus. We cannot have too high a view of God.

Just as Isaiah did, we must seek the Lord in the temple. Turn to Him, pursue Him, search for Him with all your heart. In the pages of Scripture you will see heaven opened and behold the Lord high and lifted up. Draw near to God, and He will draw near to you.

As you grow to know the true God, I assure you, you will *not* see a god made in your own image. Nor will you behold a user-friendly god slouched upon the throne. Instead, you will come to know Him who is holy, awesome, fearful, and sovereign, and who has extended His unmerited love and grace toward us in His Son, Jesus Christ.

The fundamental fact of our faith is God, and the fundamental fact about God is that He is holy. Everything rests upon this.

I repeat—*everything!*

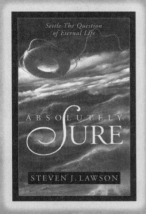